CANDLEMAKING
FOR PROFIT

CANDLEMAKING
FOR PROFIT

Eugenia (Deannie) Bourn

South Brunswick and New York: A. S. Barnes and Company
London: Thomas Yoseloff Ltd

A. S. Barnes and Co., Inc.
Cranbury, New Jersey 08512

Thomas Yoseloff Ltd
108 New Bond Street
London W1Y OQX, England

Library of Congress Cataloging in Publication Data

Bourn, Eugenia.
    Candlemaking for profit.

    Bibliography: p.
    1. Candles. 2. Self-employed. I. Title.
TT896.5.B68   745.59'3   72-9062
ISBN 0-498-01282-4

PRINTED IN THE UNITED STATES OF AMERICA

To Mother and Daddy—
who always knew I could.

Contents

Preface

In the past, when one thought of a candle, he probably thought of a slender, wax light-source that was burned maybe at romantic dinners, or whenever the electricity went off. But candles today aren't what they used to be in shape, smell, color, texture or function.

Nor do they cost the few pennies they used to. Candles, especially decorative ones, are big business. Every year people burn up hundreds of thousands of dollars in candles. Interior decorators use them extensively for accent pieces. Housewives adore them. Sweet little old ladies burn them to brighten their day or chase the blues. Candles "turn on" the teen-aged set. Young marrieds use candles instead of fussy bric-a-brac. Young singles buy unusual ones as conversation pieces. Men like big masculine-looking candles for a den or on a bar. Even *babies* get candles for birthday presents!

There are probably as many reasons for people buying candles as there are people who buy them, but one thing is certain, people *do* buy them. One gift shop near the Arlington Heights (Illinois) area expects to sell $25,000 worth of candles this year. Another shop which deals exclusively in candles, supports its two owners in style and has at least four full-time salespeople employed year around.

So, ask me why I got into the candle business, and I'll tell you to help people burn up their money. The more they burn, the more I make. Ask me how you can have money to burn, and I'll tell you how to set up your own small candle business at home. That is the purpose of this book.

I should emphasize that I mean a small, or part-time business. To gross more than $3,000 or $4,000 a year will require an entirely different approach. But if you are a homebound mother, a retired person, a student, a church group, or just someone looking for a source of extra income, I think you will find this an ideal opportunity.

Keep in mind that besides the actual money that you earn each hour, there are special tax deductions available to you; you are your own boss and work your own hours; you do not need extra clothes or to pay transportation costs to and from a regular job; and best of all, candlemaking is fun and easy to do.

I have been making candles for profit since 1968. My first order was for $20. One of my latest ones was for nearly $2,000. Needless to say, the equipment and the methods of candlemaking are very different for such different quantities. For simplicity's sake, I shall give you three stages or levels of production, named according to the type of melting equipment you will use:

1. The Double Boiler Stage—for orders up to $25
2. The Roaster Oven Stage—for orders up to $1,000 or so
3. The Big Pot Stage—for orders over $1,000

It was my good fortune to be able to begin very inexpensively and on a very small scale, and then progress gradually to large-order candle making. Nearly all of my profits were immediately put back into the business to enlarge without growing pains.

You may want to do this, or you may wish to get deeply involved, moneywise, right away. That is up to you. I shall tell you how experience taught me to handle each stage.

Eugenia L. Bourn
Deannie Candles

CANDLEMAKING
FOR PROFIT

1
Beginning Your Candle Business

If you have never made a candle before, or if your candlemaking has been limited to melting down some leftover wax and pouring it into a makeshift mold, then this chapter is where you must begin your candle business at home.

MATERIALS

1. *Wax* There are essentially two kinds of candle wax: beeswax and refined paraffin. Beeswax has many fine qualities, but it is so terribly expensive that it is not suitable for use in large, decorative candles.

Refined paraffin wax is cheap (I pay only 13.5¢ per pound for it), clean, versatile (there are paraffins with altogether different melting points and different molding and burning qualities), and it is easy to get in large quantities.

I use only one kind of paraffin for all my candles (except hurricane candles) and that is Standard Oil's Eskar-R-35 wax, which has a melting point of about 135°. Any paraffin which meets this specification will serve to make any of the candles explained later in this book.

If, however, you cannot get this wax for your first few candles, don't despair. A good hobby shop will be your first source of candle supplies, and they should be able to provide you with a similar paraffin. They will also have dyes, wicking, and molds in the small quantities you'll need to start with.

2. *Molds* You cannot expect professional-looking candles from nonprofessional molds, and although some of the candles explained herein allow the use of milk cartons and makeshift molds, I strongly recommend that

you secure professional metal molds as early as possible in your business.

Properly cared for, a good mold will give you years of service, and the beauty of a shiny candle from a metal mold cannot be matched from cardboard or plastic cartons.

The mold you choose should be made of heavy metal, carefully assembled, and slightly tapered to allow easy removal of the finished candle. Even if they look straight up and down, they should taper a bit. The more they taper, the easier you will find it is to unmold your handiwork.

Your molds should get tender loving care. Collectively, they are the biggest investment you will make, and it is important that they get good treatment to prolong their lives. Mold care will be discussed in the Double Boiler Stage.

Molds will probably come to you with a thin film of silicone spray in them. This protects the mold, gives a shiny surface to your candle, and also aids in releasing the candle. Silicone spray should only be used in a clean mold, however. Its good effects are neutralized if there is dust or debris in the mold.

Do not leave your molds in the water bath for extended periods of time. They should be taken out and dried off as soon as the candle is cool. They are metal and will rust if you aren't careful.

It isn't necessary to clean your molds every time you use them, or even every dozen times, but the time will come. There are lots of ways to skin this cat, and they are covered in the Double Boiler Stage.

The main body of your candles will probably be molded in a metal mold, but the embellishments which make the candles real decorator items often are made with plastic molds.

These are the plastic resin casting molds at your hobby shop. They all used to be made of polyethylene, but now there is butyrate plastic. The products of poly molds often were pitted or broken, but the butyrate molds turn out a design which is whole and glossy, thus eliminating the need for antiquing or other cover ups.

Also available for candle crafting are the two-piece three-dimensional candle molds with designs already incorporated into the candles. They are fascinating, and they do turn out lovely candles, but they do have a drawback—your buyers (for shops and stores, not hobby shops) do not want to try to sell a candle at retail that can be easily copied at home by every customer. If you can find molds which are sufficiently different from those shown in your area, you will be able to use them. Otherwise, I suggest that you do not use them.

Admittedly, the candles described in The Double Boiler Stage are easily copied, and many hobby shops may have some of the molds from which they are made, but the chances of all five candles being imitated in one area are very remote. Your buyer will appreciate the fact that you go "all over the country" to put together candles that are unique.

3. *Scents* First of all, if you or any members of your family have allergy problems, and you make or store your candles in the house, experiment with samples or small bottles of scent before making any large investments in this. Some people have severe allergic reactions to the pungent odors of scented candles, and if this is so with you or your family, you'd do well to skip this aspect of candlemaking.

Besides, I find that most people who want scented candles want little ones, and they don't like to pay much for them. That means that by the time you pay for wax, dye, wicking and scent for a candle (and scents *do* get expensive) and then tie a mold, pour the wax, cool the candle, unmold, level, wrap and label it, you will find there is very little profit in it. You would do better to spend that time of tying the mold, cooling, unmolding and leveling the candle on a big one that will give you greater profit.

If you do use scents, though, they may be oils or synthetics. They will come to you with instructions. Follow them and remember these things: If you put in too much scent, the candle will craze. Or if it's a white one, it may turn color and not be pure white. Also, the scents evaporate and the candle will have a shorter shelf life than its unscented neighbor.

They say that you can scent only the wick of your candle, or you can fill the well with heavily scented wax, but the most efficient method is to add the scent to the melted wax just before pouring the candle.

4. *Dyes* Wax must be colored with oil dyes. Food colors, water paints, etc., will not combine with the wax and therefore will not color it. Oil paints are too expensive, and they're a lot of trouble. Crayons have a tendency to settle, and sometimes they are treated with material that not only will not burn, but may even put out the flame.

Your best bet for dyes is actual candle dyes. You will use different kinds of dyes at different stages in your business. The cheapest and best types for each stage will be covered in discussing these.

5. *Wicking* Commercial wicking comes in different sizes according to how many threads are used to braid it. Some of it is braided flat, some round, and some around a metal center that holds the burning wick up out of the well of wax, which would extinguish it, should it fall over.

The size wicking you use depends on the size candle you are making. Probably the manufacturer of your mold will supply you with the proper-sized wicking for each candle. You should follow their suggestions until you feel confident enough to experiment with larger or smaller wicks or wicks of other substances than thread.

You will get up to 40% discounts over hobby store prices by purchasing in quantity, but if you can use several thousand yards of each type, you can try buying from Atkins and Pearce, Pike and Pearl Streets, Cincinnati, Ohio, the only wick manufacturer I could find in the entire United States.

I use wicking from two sources, Pourette and American Handicrafts. You may want to try these.

6. *Stearic acid* Stearine or stearic acid is a fatty acid which is sometimes used in candlemaking. An excerpt from *The Modern Art of Candle Creating* explains its function:

> The addition of stearic acid to paraffin does not raise the melting point of the wax, but does improve the burning quality and makes a harder and stronger candle. Stearic acid itself forms a hard crystal which forms a matrix within the candle, furnishing a resistant framework. By making the candle harder and stronger, the candle also becomes longer burning. In addition, stearic acid tends to make the candle more opaque.*

Most of my candles do not contain stearic acid. I seek the soft glow of a candle to emphasize the designs I have put on it, and I do not wish it to be opaque. I have also discovered that the presence of stearic acid in candles causes some gold or metallic paints used for highlights to tarnish.

If you want to experiment with stearic acid, you may buy it from the large industrial chemical companies (try Armour) for about 79¢ per pound plus freight in quantities under 200 pounds. If you can use more than 200 pounds, the price drops to 29¢ per pound, and they'll pay the delivery costs.

---

*Don Olsen, *The Modern Art of Candle Creating* (A. S. Barnes and Co.: South Brunswick and New York, 1964), p.9.

2

The Double Boiler Stage

Now that you have a general idea about the materials used in candlemaking, you are ready to actually begin candlemaking in the Double Boiler Stage.

I started my candle business in my kitchen with a double boiler, a slab of paraffin, a wad of candle dye, 2 yards of wicking, a quart milk carton, some resin casting molds, an instruction book, and lots of determination. I would call this an absolute minimum of equipment.

Following are some suggestions for equipment which I think you will need to run your candle business at nearly all levels.

1. *Melting Pot* At first you will probably want to make only one or two candles at a time, and any ordinary double boiler will do nicely. It isn't absolutely necessary that you use a double boiler, but it's safer. Any wax melted directly over a flame can and will burst into flame unless it is carefully watched. It's a rather frightening experience.

If your wax *should* catch fire, first try to cover the pot it is in. This cuts off the oxygen so that it cannot continue to burn. If you cannot do this, keep bicarbonate of soda handy to throw on the flame or use a fire extinguisher. Do not put water on a wax fire, it only spreads the flames.

If you do not have a double boiler and do not wish to invest in one, place your pot in a tray of water, and then heat.

2. *Fire extinguisher* Better safe than sorry—and keep it mounted on the wall or someplace where it's handy to your melting area.

A hand fire extinguisher usually costs around $10 or so. Besides, your insurance company will undoubtedly require it to underwrite your homeowners or fire insurance policy.

3. *Candy or deep fat thermometer* Most candles will be poured at about 190°, but glass and plastic molds may be destroyed by such high

heat—165° to 180° is better. You will find that this thermometer is a useful tool. Using it can save you time and money.

4. *Pouring device* Rather than pouring directly from your melting pot, you will probably find it helpful to have a large metal pitcher or teakettle to pour from. I used a Pyrex measuring cup to ladle the wax into a gallon aluminum pitcher. Then I poured my largest candles all in one stream from it.

If you are pouring very small molds or small candles, it may be quicker and less messy to pour directly from a measuring cup.

As you develop your own candles, you will know exactly how many ounces or cups it takes to fill each mold to the desired capacity, and by using these measurements, you can save yourself time and money.

5. *Mold Sealer* When you use metal molds with wick holes, you will need to seal the hole to keep the melted wax in and the water bath out.

If the metal molds you buy don't come equipped with tiny screws, by all means purchase some from the nearest hardware store. And while you are there, pick up a roll of caulking cord, the type used to seal windows from inside in the winter. It makes a great mold sealer, is reusable, and only costs a dollar or two for a big roll. The hobby suppliers have essentially the same thing for sale for a nickel a plug. It doesn't take many plugs to amount to a dollar or two.

6. *Mold weights* After the candle is poured (metal mold) the mold must be immersed in cool water up to the level of the wax. Because wax is lighter than water, the mold will tip and spill if it isn't weighted.

One way to do this is to make a collar of lead weights or pipe to go over the metal mold and weight it from the bottom.

If you don't care to invest in these underwater weights, you may use clean bricks, old bleach and detergent bottles filled with water, or nearly anything flat and heavy to lay across the top of the mold to hold it under the water and keep it from tipping while the candle cools.

7. *Cooling vats* Plastic buckets, wastebaskets, large laundry tubs, a deep sink, even garbage cans—anything with a flat bottom that will hold water and not rust is satisfactory for this. These vats will be filled with water to the proper depth, and the candles will be cooled in them. The water bath gives a shiny finish to the candle.

8. *Refrigerator* It is possible to remove the hardened candle from the mold without chilling it first, but it's much faster and easier to get out if it's cold.

While in the double boiler stage, you can use your family refrigerator (*Note:* don't ever freeze your candles), but as you progress to the Roaster Oven Stage, you'll need lots more cooling space.

I watched the classified ads until I found an ancient refrigerator for

$25, and I use it to cool my candles. I think you'll find it well worth the investment.

9. *Stove or hot plate* After the candles come out of the molds, they will be rough on the bottom and maybe not exactly the size you want them. Heat an old cast iron frying pan on a hot plate, stove or even a camp stove, and hold the candle in it until the bottom is smooth and the candle is the height you desire. Be sure to get a frying pan large enough to accommodate the diameter of the largest candle mold you have.

If the wax accumulates in the pan enough to spoil the sides of the candle, remove the candle from the pan and pour the accumulated wax into another container. Then return the candle to the heated pan.

Oh, and for family harmony and health, don't let your candle pan get into your pantry. One day I had blown a fuse in the basement and couldn't use my hot plate, so I came upstairs to the kitchen stove to level some candles. When I finished, I left the frying pan there to cool. It had only a thin film of wax remaining in it.

I was busy and forgot the pan, and the next thing I knew, my husband, seeking a snack, was warming a piece of steak in there. He wasn't too happy with the wax coating he got on his meat!

10. *X-acto or craft knives* Almost indispensable! I use them to cut up my dyes or shave off just the tiniest piece of dye for light colors. Also, after the candles come out of the molds, the wick is cut with an x-acto knife. Then, too, when you level your candles in the warm frying pan, the wick will prohibit proper melting. Gouge out as much of the wick as you can with the sharp point of the knife so that the candle bottom will melt down evenly. I also measure the desired height of each candle on every side and make a mark or a notch with the knife so I know when it's short enough.

Use these knives also to shave off the mold seam after the candle is finished.

11. *Cooling pans* Cake or cookie pans, even muffin tins will receive excess wax when you have made too much of one color. Also, they are handy to pour the colored wax into when you're making chunk candles. When the wax is cool enough, slice it with a knife or putty knife into chunks of the desired size.

12. *Electric drill* If this is not available, a couple of ice picks will do. Many of the candles you may make will be wicked (wikt) after they are cooled. An electric drill with a sturdy piece of large diameter wire for a bit will zip right through this job. If you don't have a drill and don't feel like buying one, a heated ice pick and a piece of flannel will do just as well.

13. *Miscellaneous*

a. *Woodburning tool* Sometimes this is used to apply designs to candles or to weld a wax shape to the main candle (e.g. sculptured wax flowers).

b. *Small paintbrushes* Buy cheap ones because you're going to put them into hot wax.

c. *Putty knife* Use this to remove mold sealer after cooling the candle —also good to put up wax chunks with. You'll probably want to buy an extra wide one for scraping up spilled wax off the floor of your work area.

d. *Hammer and chisel* These are for breaking up slabs of wax so that they fit into your melting pot.

When you have secured the preceding articles of equipment, you are ready to go find a hobby shop, buy a mold, some wax, dye, and wicking, and start making candles.

I shall assume that there is some kind of a craft or hobby shop near you from which you can purchase your supplies. Check with them first for molds, etc., at this stage, and if they don't have what you need, you may order from the companies I use. My suppliers are all mentioned for each candle, and are also listed in the back of the book.

3

Best-Selling Candle Ideas

The following step-by-step procedures will help you make some of the candles that have been best sellers for me.

FLEURETTES OR ROSETTES

This candle is basically a 3-inch cube of wax with appliqués on the sides and tops. You may use a milk carton to mold the body of the candle, or you may order a 3-inch square mold from Pourette Mfg. (See List of Suppliers).

If you use a metal mold, there will be wick hole. To tie the mold, first cut a piece of wicking 10 to 12 inches longer than you need. This is so that when the candle is finished and the wick is cut off at the 3-inch mark, you will have plenty of wicking left to tie 2 or 3 other candles. If you make it only long enough to tie one candle, it will be too short to tie the next mold, and several inches will be wasted. This way you don't throw away a piece but once every 4 or 5 candles. Incidentally, save every scrap of your wicking. You'll be surprised at how a couple of inches can sometimes make a candle!

If I seem penny conscious, it's because I am, and you must be too! Every penny you spend to make, package, and sell your candles cuts into your profit. Don't scrimp to sacrifice quality, but when you can save a penny or two on each candle, do it. Pretty soon you'll have saved a dollar, or many dollars.

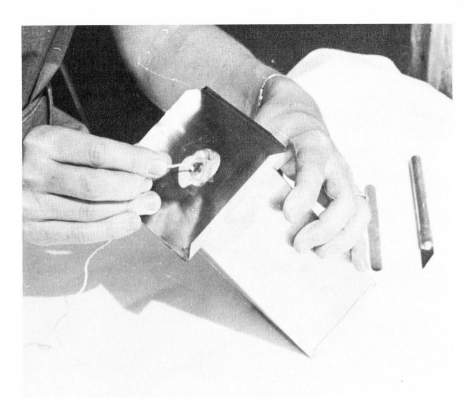

FIG. 1 *Thread the wick through the hole*

FIG. 2 *Seal wick hole with retainer screw*

FIG. 3 *Caulking compound procedure*

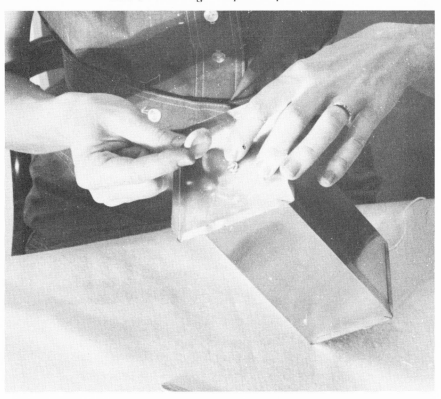

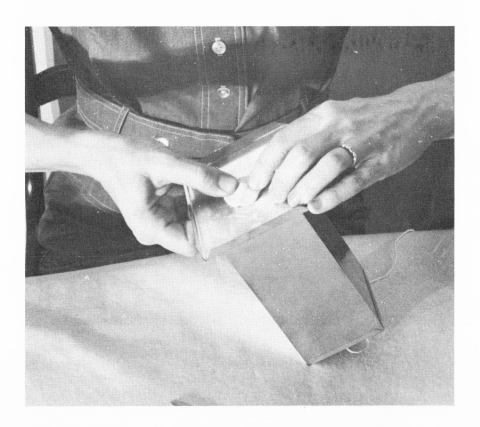

When the wick is cut, turn the mold so that the wick hole is toward you and thread the wick through the hole (Fig. 1).

Seal the wick hole with a tiny retainer screw (pan head tapping screw, ¼ x 6). Twist this in with the fingers only. Using a screwdriver may damage the mold, or at best cut the wick (Fig. 2). Then seal the wick hole area with caulking compound (Fig. 3) such as Mortite Weather-strip and Caulking Cord by Mortell Co., Kankakee, Illinois.

Most of the candle supply companies offer mold sealer for sale, but caulking compound is much cheaper, and it can be used over and over again. When at last it gets dirty, toss it out. Don't attempt to clean it.

Turn the mold over so that the open end is up. Make a slip knot (Fig. 4) and put a popsicle stick through it (Fig. 5).

Lay the popsicle stick across the top of the mold and loop excess wicking around one end so that it gets into neither the water nor the wax (Fig. 6).

Pour the candle so that it is about 4 inches deep in the mold. You want it deeper than the finished height to allow for shrinkage, filling, and leveling.

I mentioned before that measuring your wax could save you time and money. If, when you are ready to pour your candle, you will try this simple trick, you will know exactly how much wax to put into each mold to turn out the size candle you want.

Put the melted wax into a measuring cup. Insert a ruler into the mold so that it touches the bottom of the mold, and then pour the wax 4 inches deep on your ruler (Fig. 7). Notice how much wax was used out of the measuring cup. This is how much wax will be needed to pour each candle the same height.

If you don't measure, you'll find yourself pouring too much or too little wax into the mold. Then, when the candle is unmolded, it will be either too short (toss it back into the pot) or too tall (this can be leveled off, but it takes a lot more time than you would have spent to measure

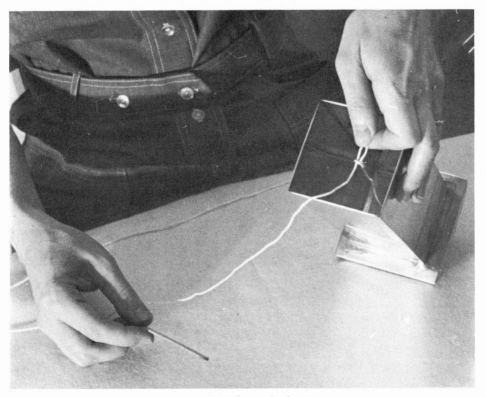

FIG. 4 *Make a slipknot*

FIG. 5 *Insert stick into knot*

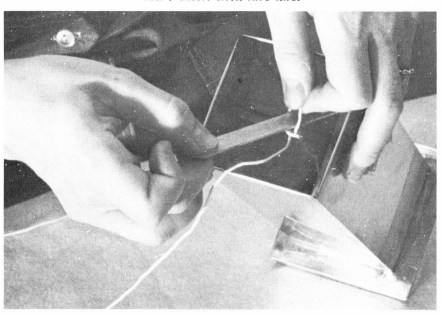

your wax as you poured). It may help you to know that it takes about 2½ cups of melted wax to equal one pound.

Now back to the pouring of our candle. All the instruction books I have ever read say to fill the "well"* as the wax cools and while it is still in the mold. When making short candles, I personally prefer to wait until the candle has been unmolded to fill the well because of the danger of an overfill (i.e. If wax overflows the well, it will seep between the mold the candle. This is called an overfill). An overfill makes it very difficult to

---

* As wax cools, it shrinks, and you will see your lovely, level candle sink inside itself, leaving a well or opening around its core. This is normal and correctible.

FIG. 6 *Loop excess wicking around stick*

remove the candle. This technique works best on short candles. Very tall ones are better filled while they're cooling in the mold.

After pouring, put the candle in a water bath to cool (Fig. 8). Be sure to weight it down with something so that it doesn't float and tip.

When it is cool, take it out of the water bath, remove the popsicle stick, mold sealer, and retainer screw (Figs. 9, 10. You may use a screw-driver or putty knife now), and put the mold and candle into the re-frigerator to cool.

To unmold the candle, pry the top of the mold gently open with your fingers (Fig. 11) until you hear the sides of the candle pop free. Then upend the candle and tap the mold firmly on a padded surface (Fig. 12)

FIG. 7 *Measuring wax*

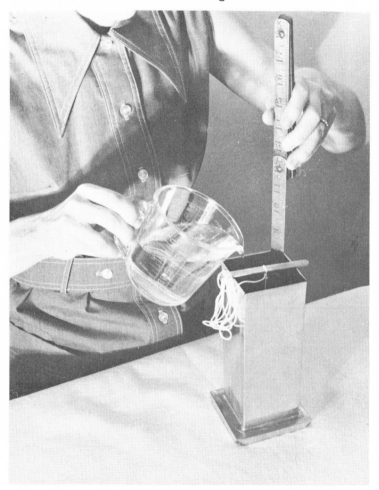

FIG. 8 *Water bath*

such as folded newspaper or toweling. Gently pull the candle out of the mold (Fig. 13).

To fill the well, unmold the candle, cut the wick off at the bottom of the candle (Fig. 14), pour in hot wax (Fig. 15), poke with an ice pick (you may have to do this before you pour, as well as after). Fill again if necessary. Allow the candle to cool.

Next you are ready to level the candle. Measure 3 inches for the top of the candle, make a notch with an x-acto knife on all four corners at the desired height (Fig. 16). Stand the candle up in a warm frying pan or on a griddle (Fig. 17) so that it melts down to 3 inches tall. As you melt, the wick may become exposed. Dig it out with the point of the x-acto knife so that you can continue melting until the desired height is obtained.

If you use a milk carton, simply pour a quart carton 4 inches full of wax, fill the well as the candle cools, allow to cool, peel the carton off the candle. Don't worry that it isn't shiny and pretty. It will be antiqued anyway. After unmolding, level as described above. Then wick the candle.

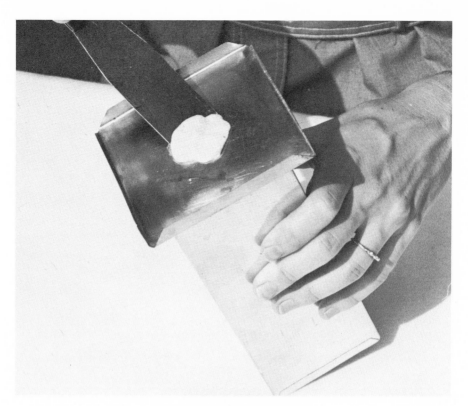

FIG. 9 *Removing mold sealer*

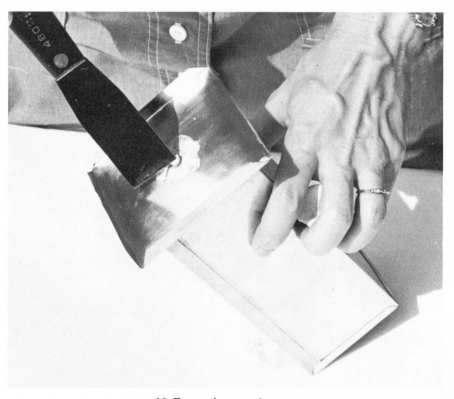

FIG. 10 *Removing retainer screw*

FIG. 11 *Pry top of mold open gently*

FIG. 12 *Tap mold on padded surface*

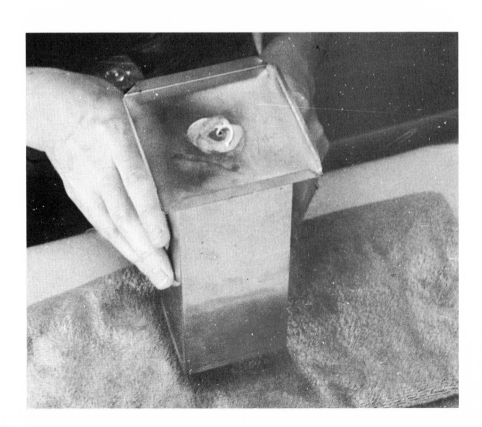

To wick a hardened candle, either use an electric drill (Fig. 18) with a 7-inch piece of heavy wire (¼-inch in diameter) for a bit, or heat an ice pick (Fig. 19) and make a hole big enough to accommodate the wick you are using. Then dip the wick in hot wax, let it cool so it is stiff, and poke it into the hole. Fill the hole around the wick with a few drops of hot wax from a glass eye dropper (plastic ones may melt when you put them in hot wax).

Now you're ready to decorate the candle.

The Fleurette design may be bought from any American Handicrafts store, item #6049–98 (four on one for about $1).

The Rosette design comes from California Titan (see List of Suppliers) and is on a large sheet with several other molds. You probably will have to buy the whole sheet, and the cost per mold is several times that of the Floret.

Actually, any mold which is 3 inches in diameter or less will suit your needs. Check at your hobby supplier.

Cut the plastic molds apart and prop them (Fig. 20). This means

FIG. 13 *Pull the candle out of the mold*

FIG. 14 *Cut the wick off at the bottom of the candle*

FIG. 15 *Pour in hot wax*

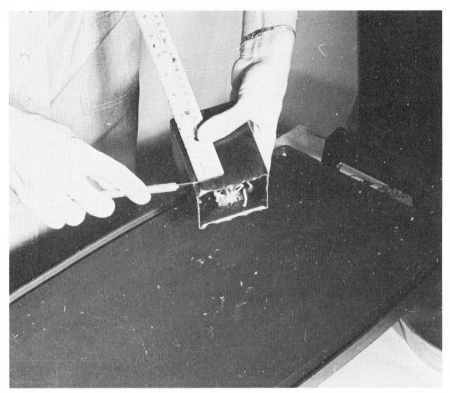

FIG. 16 *Notch with a knife at correct height*

FIG. 17 *Melt excess wax off on a griddle or in a frying pan*

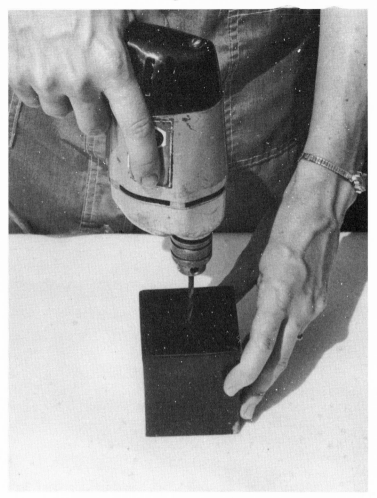

FIG. 18 *Wicking the candle with an electric drill*

to find a jar, box, pan or something that will allow the mold to seat itself in the opening, but the edges are supported by the sides of the jar or whatever. I use square plastic freezer containers to prop my designs, but don't feel constrained to copy. A coffee cup, a pudding cup or jello mold, a tin can will serve your purpose just as well.

Or you can use the method I use for big, big orders, the sandbox method (Fig. 21). Get an inch or two of sand in a box or large, flat container of some kind, snuggle the molds down in it, pour the wax in them, and adjust until they are level. Fill, and allow to cool.

It will take five designs to complete the candle—one for the top, and one for each of the four sides. You may have to make two pourings. It's

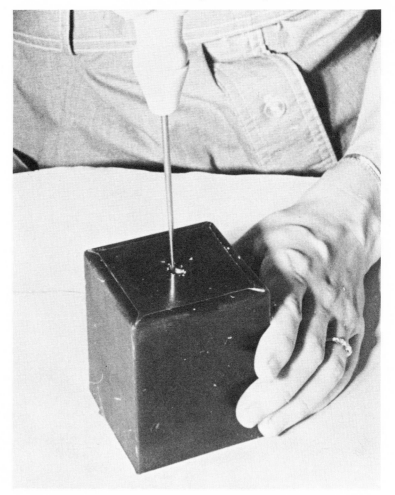

FIG. 19 *Wicking the candle with a hot ice pick*

a good idea to pour one or two extra in case one of the designs breaks while being unmolded.

After cooling, chill the designs and remove them from the molds. Minor flaws will be covered by the last step, antiquing.

To remove the applique designs from the molds, gently peel back the plastic and apply pressure to the center of the mold with your thumb (Fig. 22).

To apply the designs to the sides of the candle, melt a small quantity of the same color wax—you may use what's left over from leveling. Position the design with your hand. Dip a small paint brush into the hot wax (not too hot, it will flame up) and paint around the edge of the

FIG. 20 *Propping the mold*

FIG. 21 *Propping the mold in sand*

FIG. 22 *Unmolding appliqué designs*

FIG. 23 *Brush hot wax around the design*

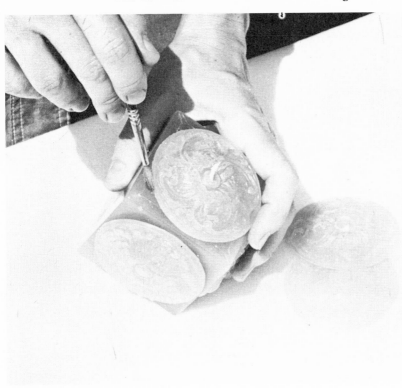

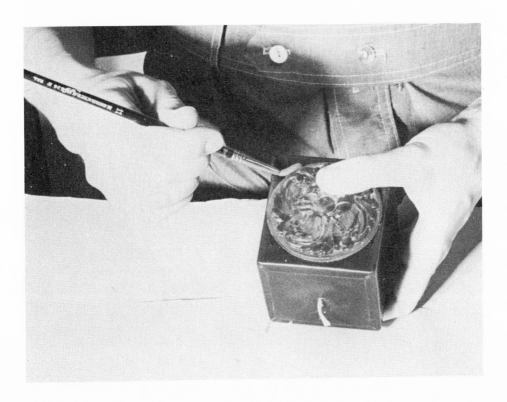

FIG. 24 *Poke a hole for the wick*

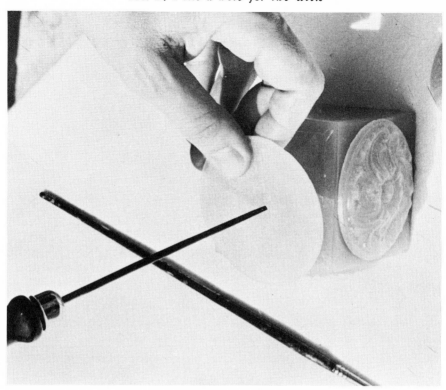

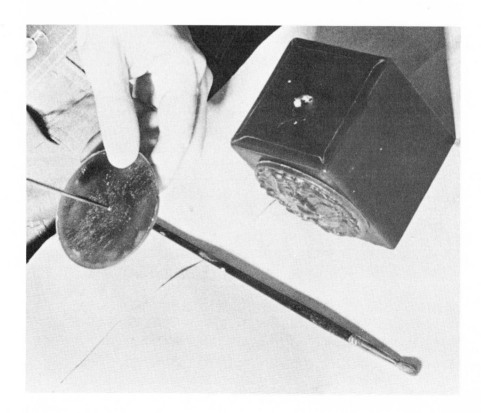

design with the hot wax (Fig. 23). This will weld the design to the side. Go all the way around each design on all four sides.

For the top, heat an ice pick, and from the back side of the design (you'll have to "guesstimate" the center point) poke a hole for the wick (Fig. 24). You must go from the back side of the mold, or the excess melted wax will spoil the design.

Thread the wick up through the hole you have just made and "paint" the top design on just as you did the sides (Fig. 25).

When the candle is completely assembled, you will want either to antique it with Amco Folk Art Antiquing Glaze (from American Handicrafts) or highlight it with Rub 'n Buff, Treasure Jewels, or one of the metallic waxes.

To antique, paint on glaze (Fig. 26) and immediately rub off all but what is in the grooves (Fig. 27). Use a circular motion on the corners of the candles to go with the circular design. Allow to dry, and the candle is finished.

Your molds, especially the metal ones, are probably the greatest investment you will make in your small candle business. Therefore, prolonging their life is important to you.

Your molds probably won't need cleaning every time you use them, or even every dozen times, but the time will come when they will need cleaning. There are lots of ways to skin this cat.

The easiest method is to pour the next candle with extra hot wax and fill the mold nearly to the top. That melts away and absorbs any accumulation that might be there, and it usually will clean the mold pretty effectively.

Or you can preheat your oven to 170° or less, turn it *off*, line a cookie pan with thick newspapers, lay the mold on its side on the papers (tilt the bottom of the mold up slightly, so that the wax can run out). Close the oven for 12–15 minutes, and let the wax inside and outside the mold run down and be absorbed by the newspapers. Do *not* forget and leave the oven on, or let it get hotter than 170°, because the solder in the mold will melt, and you'll have a sieve instead of a candle mold when you're finished.

Also, when you are finished, put on a cooking mitt or something to protect your hands, and swish out the bottom of the oven while it's still warm with a couple of paper towels. They'll pick up any stray drops of wax, and may save you a very smoky kitchen, or even a fire, the next time you try to cook in there.

Wax in a dirty mold can be removed chemically with chlorothene. It's effective, but expensive. Close the wick hole with mold sealer, or hold your finger over it. Then pour four or five ounces of *chlorothene* in the

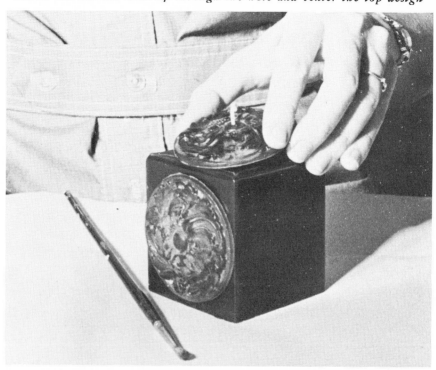

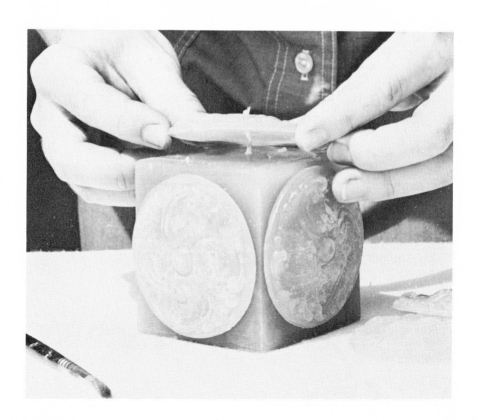

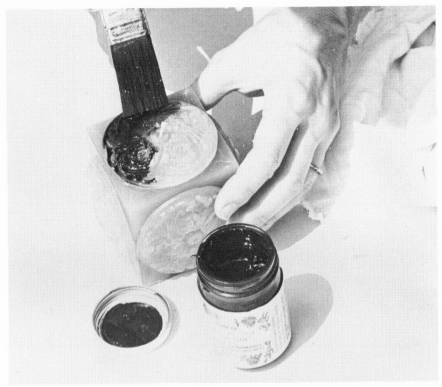

FIG. 26 *Paint on antiquing glaze*

mold, and swish it around. You may have to swab down the sides of the mold with a king-sized swab or a rag on a stick, or something to get it all. Then pour the whole mess out, and allow the mold to dry thoroughly before using.

Finally, here is my favorite way of cleaning molds. It's such a Rube Goldberg method, that I'm almost ashamed to tell it to you, but the chemical method is expensive, and I ruined six molds one day because I forgot and left the oven on, and the extra-hot wax method isn't entirely effective, so here goes.

First clean them as best you can with the extra hot pouring of a candle. Just after you pour the hot wax, wipe the *outside* down with some paper towels to get any wax off the exterior. Then cool the candle and remove it from the mold.

Now you have a nearly clean mold. Set your hot water heater to maximum heat. It ought to be there anyway, if you have a dishwasher. Run that 160° water into the mold. (You probably will want to wear heavy cotton-lined rubber gloves for this procedure as that water gets

FIG. 27 *Rub off excess glaze*

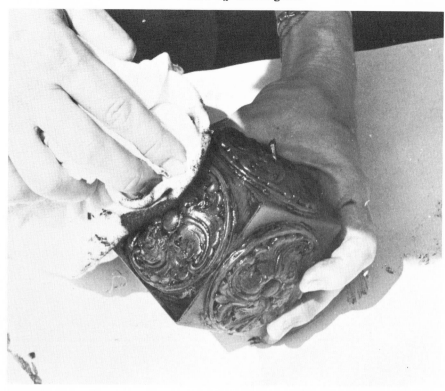

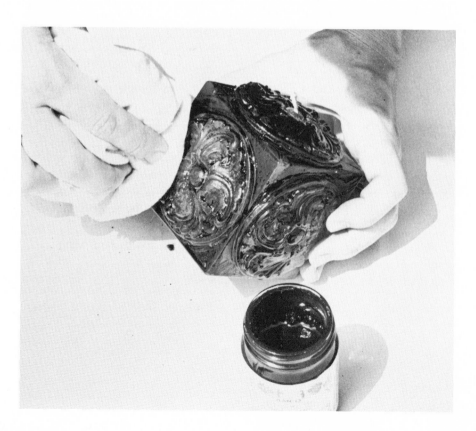

really hot.) It will melt any remaining wax, float it to the top, and run it out the drain (my plumber is probably gleefully rubbing his hands at the prospect of all this wax in my drains, but I've done it this way for nearly three years with no ill effects). I don't recommend that you allow large quantities of melted wax (or even cooled wax) down your drains, but a little bit now and then doesn't seem to hurt.

Next you must dry your mold thoroughly, or it will rust. If it's big enough to reach into, you can wrap a towel or soft rag around your hand and dry it out just like drying dishes, but if it's narrow or oddly shaped, take the hood off of a home hair dryer, or put the blower attachment on a vacuum cleaner, run the hose down into the mold, and turn it on. Warm air will dry it quickly.

Do you see now why I hesitated to tell you this one?

When your molds are not in use, keep them covered with a plastic bag. You have also just used a rather intricate plastic, resin casting mold to make the wax decorations for your candle. Probably there are a few small pieces of wax clinging to the inside of the mold. This should be cleaned out before using the mold again. It cannot be done by pouring extra hot wax in the molds or putting them in the oven (they will melt).

You should pick out the wax you can with your fingernail or an orange stick, taking care not to gouge the plastic. Then hold them under very hot running water until all vestiges of wax are gone. Dry thoroughly with a towel or soft cloth.

The Fleurette or Rosette is made to sell for $4, so you should expect a wholesale price of $2. If that seems like too much work for less than $2 profit, let me just say that it isn't a very big profit, but many times a small candle sells better than a larger one, and making these by the dozen greatly cuts down on the actual time spent working on each candle.

I can completely finish a dozen Fleurettes in 3 to 3½ hours, a profit of $3 per hour. It all depends on proficiency, which you will pick up as you go along.

The next two candles are variations on a theme, but they get progressively larger, sell for more money, and require very little more work than the smaller appliquéd candles.

MAGIC

This candle is made from a 4-inch square hurricane mold (i.e. it has no wick hole), which may be bought from American Handicrafts or Pourette, and five appliqued designs, the molds for which are available from California Titan.

FIG. 28 *Melt off ends of appliqués so they will fit the top of the candle*

This candle is poured and assembled just like a Fleurette except:

1. The body of the candle will be 4x4x4½ inches.

2. The designs are about 4½ inches tall so when you get ready to put one on the top, you will have to melt off a fraction of an inch on the two long ends of the design so it will fit the 4x4 top (Fig. 28).

3. Use Pourette's large metal core wicking for this candle.

4. These designs are usually bumpy and irregular on the back. Place each one, backside-down in a warm frying pan momentarily, and melt it off until it's flat an˙ smooth It will apply much easier, and look better (Fig. 28).

5. The weight of these designs requires a different type of application from the smaller candles. ınstead of painting them on with hot wax, lay the body of the candle flat on a table, or hold in your lap, and place the design where you want it to go. Then take a wood-burning tool or electric pencil and˙ olding it at about a 45° angle, run it along the sides of the

design so that both the design and the body of the candle melt together and form a weld (Fig. 29).

6. You do not have to prop these design molds, but use a level table to pour on.

If the Pourette large metal core wicking and Eskar R-35 wax is used for this candle, it will burn a well about 2 inches in diameter down the center of the candle. It will not drip.

If you use some other size or type of wicking, you will have to test the candle by burning it before you try to sell it. Your buyers usually want to know how the candles burn.

After antiquing or highlighting, this candle will sell for $5.50 retail, which gives you a price of $2.75 wholesale.

MEDALLION

The body of this candle is made from a 5-inch square hurricane mold.

FIG. 29 *Applying appliqué with a wood-burning tool*

These may be obtained from Deep Flex, Premier Manufacturing, or custom made from Pourette. The designs may be bought from Deep Flex, or one of their distributors.

If you order a dozen or more, there is no extra charge for having the molds drawn in Butyrate plastic, which is far superior to the old polyethylene molds. The butyrate plastic turns out a perfect wax design every time, no chips, no pits, and it will be very shiny and pretty. Using these molds eliminates the need for antiquing, which saves you time and money.

Make a 5-inch cube of wax, fill and level. Pour five designs. Wick the candle using Pourette's extra metal core wicking. Apply the designs either by painting on with hot wax or welding with a wood-burning tool.

This candle requires no antiquing if butyrate molds are used. If you use polypropylene molds, you will probably have to cover up the flaws they leave in the wax by antiquing or highlighting. You will have to prop the molds for appliqués. I use two-pound coffee cans or sand.

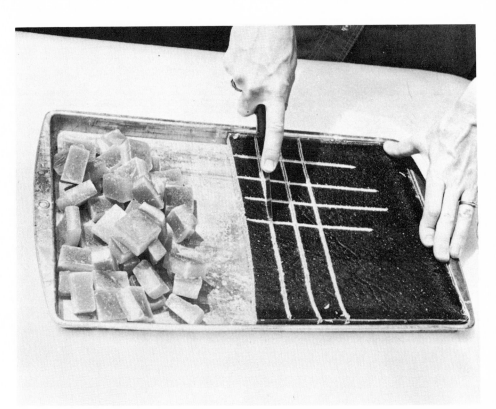

FIG. 30 *Cutting chunks of wax for a heavenly sphere*

1.

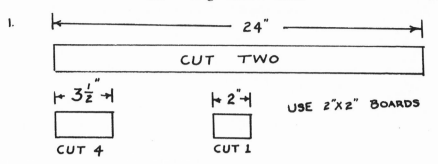

24"

CUT TWO

3½" — CUT 4

2" — CUT 1

USE 2"X2" BOARDS

2.

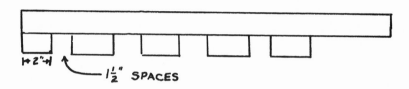

2" 1½" SPACES

3

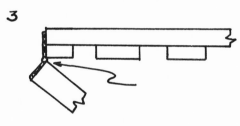

4.

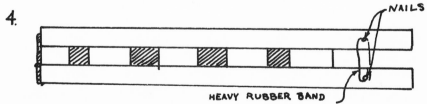

NAILS

HEAVY RUBBER BAND

HEAVENLY SPHERE

This is probably the easiest and fastest candle to make, and, happily, the one that sells the best.

It is a chunk candle, spherical in form, and I make it in two main color combinations: one with pastel chunks of wax in white, and the other with avocado, orange, and brown wax chunks in yellow.

Begin this candle with a 5-inch diameter spherical glass mold. These are available in nearly all hobby shops for about 50¢ apiece. I buy them by the case of 70 and pay slightly under 36¢ each for them.

Now make your wax chunks. There are at least two ways of doing this. My preferred way is to color enough wax to fill a cookie tray. Make pale pink, green, yellow, aqua, blue, and lavender. When the wax is almost completely cooled, it will be soft and pliable, but firm enough to hold together in a chunk when it is cut apart (Fig. 30).

The second method is to allow the wax to cool completely in the pans. Then it may be cut into chunks with a power saw or broken into small pieces with a hammer and a chisel.

These candles may be cooled in one of two ways: air cooled or cooled in a water bath.

If you cannot or do not wish to make a cooling rack and vat for your spheres, and you do not mind a few very minor frost marks on top of the candles, you may simply pour the candles and sit them upright on an empty tin can to air cool (Fig. 31). If you want a flawless, shiny-all-over sphere, you will want to prepare a water bath for it to cool in.

I bought some troughlike metal flower planters which measure 24x8x5½ inches. Then I made a rack to hold the molds upright and to weight them down in the water. You will have to adapt this cooling rack to fit your cooling vat, but mine was made like this:

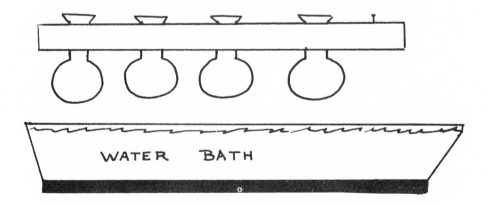

WATER   BATH

If you cut your chunks before they are cold, take a flexible putty knife and cut the soft wax into chunks just small enough to go into the glass mold. Keep them as large as possible to prevent their melting when the hot wax is poured around them. Then give the chunks a chance to cool thoroughly.

Drop all six colors of chunks at random into the glass mold until the round part is full (Fig. 32). It isn't necessary to fill the neck of the mold with chunks. Then pour white wax into the mold and allow to cool. Be sure to pour the wax about 1 inch up into the neck of the mold to allow for shrinkage.

A 10% addition of stearic acid adds to the beauty of this pastel candle because it makes the wax appear whiter, but the stearine does cut down the

FIG. 31 *Air-cooling the sphere*

glow qualities of the candle, so it isn't as pretty when it burns. Try it both ways, and see which one you like better.

Hold the mold upright until it cools, either in a water bath or empty can.

If you can see a well hole to fill after the candle has cooled, fill it, but if not, you may do it at a later stage.

When the wax is thoroughly cool and the well, if any, has been filled, place the candles in the refrigerator to cool. When they are chilled, break away the glass mold (Figs. 33 and 34). I always wear protective goggles to keep flying glass out of my eyes.

Wipe the candle with paper toweling to get rid of all slivers of glass (Fig. 35). Then level off the excess inch or so of wax that was in the neck of the mold (Fig. 36). Allow it to flatten into a base about 1½ inches in diameter on the bottom of the candle. Now all of the candle is

FIG. 32 *Filling the mold with wax chunks*

spherical except a 1½-inch flat spot on the bottom which makes a base for the candle to sit on. If a well appears as you melt off the excess wax, fill it and sit the candle upside down in a tin can to cool.

To wick the candle, follow one of these 2 methods.

1. *Electric drill* Using a heavy wire or a very small, round file for a bit, drill about 4 inches into the candle. Put a piece of Pourette's large metal core wick in the hole. Use a glass eye dropper to carefully fill the hole with hot wax. As the first bit of wax is dropped in, slide the wick up and down in the hole once or twice to help the hot wax get all the way down into the wick hole and hold the wick secure.

2. *Hot ice pick* Heat an ice pick so it is red hot. Hold a piece of flannel or soft cloth right next to the place where the hole is to be made. This will absorb the melted wax, which will flow out when the hot pick is poked into the candle. Plunge the hot ice pick into the center of the sphere to form a wick hole (Fig. 37).

Insert the wick and refill the wick hole with an eye dropper or two

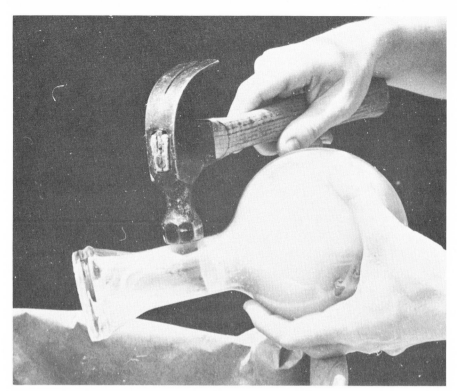

FIG. 33 *Breaking the glass mold*

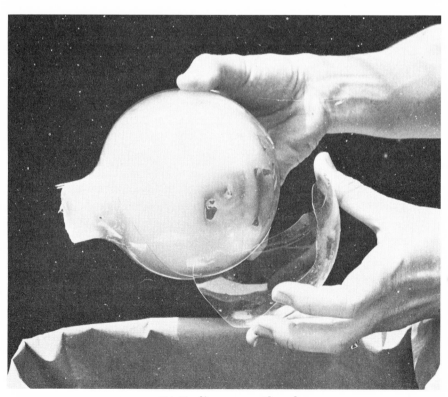

FIG. 34 *Peeling away the glass*

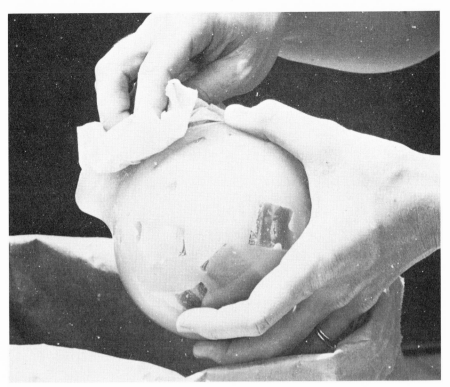

FIG. 35 *Wipe away excess glass with a paper towel*

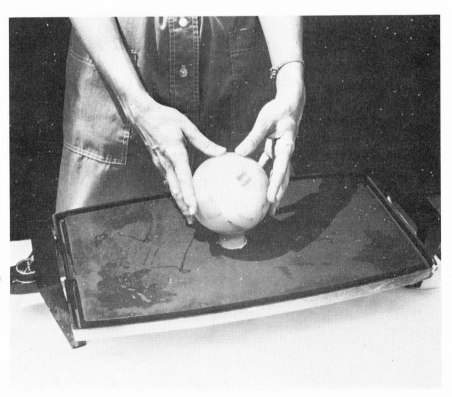

FIG. 36 *Leveling the sphere*

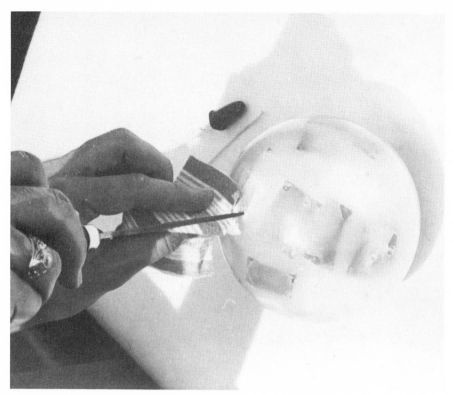

FIG. 37 *Wicking the candle with a hot ice pick*

FIG. 38 *Fill in wick hole with hot wax dropped from an eye dropper*

of hot wax. Be careful not to let the wax drip down the side (Fig. 38).

The other sphere is made the same way, except that bright yellow wax is poured over avocado, orange, and brown chunks.

The real beauty of this candle is in its burning, and it is essential that your buyer and his sales people know how it burns in order for them to sell it. As the candle burns, a well about 2–2½ inches in diameter will form. The wick will burn right down through the candle without dripping. The deeper it burns, the more the colorful wax chunks will glow in front of the flame. After all of the existing wick has been consumed, a small votive candle may be dropped into the wick well so that the candle can be used again and again.

It does seem to help sales to attach a small card to each candle explaining how it burns. In a couple of stores, it has meant the difference in the candle's selling or not. It did not sell before the notes were attached, but sold out again and again when the customers were told how it would burn.

During the Christmas season, a white heavenly sphere with bright red and green chunks in it sells rather well. If these are scented with pine or bayberry, it helps sell them.

When you pour the hot white wax over the red and green chunks, you will notice a bleeding of the dyes. This can ruin the candle, so I recommend that when strong colors such as these are used, the chunks should be chilled to very cold and the wax poured over them at no more than 175–180°F.

Another word of caution: Do not make these candles up more than a few weeks ahead of the season, as the color in the chunks tends to bleed, even after the candle is made. It is only noticeable after two or three months, and then it is a gradual process, but you and your buyer should know that these Christmas spheres have a shelf life of approximately three or four months.

Before you try to sell your candles, you should know exactly how they will burn. Burning qualities of a candle are affected by a great many things: the kind of paraffin used, the size of wicking, the size of the candle itself, whether it is burned in a draft, whether it is burned against a cold wall or window, and many other factors.

My buyers usually ask me how a candle burns, whether it smokes or drips, etc. So, I must have thoroughly tested each style to be able to answer their questions.

Most of the Deannie Candles will burn a well down the center of the candle and not drip, but the smaller ones will only do that if they are burned no more than 1–1½ hours at a time. These are things you will need to learn about your candles.

If, after you have tested a candle, you are not satisfied with its burning qualities, try a variation such as a larger or smaller wick, a different type of wax, or additives until you get exactly what you are after.

When you know how to make saleable candles and how each of them will burn, you are ready to price your candles for marketing.

The magic number for pricing seems to be $5. Any decorative candle of any appreciable size, which sells for $5 or under seems to sell better than bigger candles, which, while they are more expensive, might be a better value. Why? Who knows? I surmise that $5 is the limit many people set on gifts. Or, if they are buying for themselves, many people blanch at burning up more than $5 in one spot. Whatever the reason, try to keep your prices below $5 on at least some of your candles.

I like to figure my candle prices in this way: Let us take the heavenly sphere for example.

First I figure the cost of all my materials:

Wax—2 lbs. @12½¢/lb. = 25¢

Wicking and dye—approximately 10¢

Mold—of course you can use the glass molds only once, but even metal and plastic molds wear out, and some consideration should be given to this when you figure your cost. The glass mold costs about 36¢ apiece.

Label—2¢

Packaging—tissue paper, newsprint, boxes enclosures, 15¢

I next decide how much my time is worth, how long it takes me to make each candle, and price it accordingly.

When you have determined the cost of your materials, you will have to decide how much your time is worth. A sales clerk in a department store makes about $1.75 per hour, a teacher $5–6 per hour, a plumber $11–12 per hour. What is your time worth to you?

Of course actual production time does not include the hours you will spend seeing buyers, keeping books, delivering candles, or developing new candles, but that will take care of itself, as you shall see.

My time is worth $3 an hour to me. So, I make and package about a dozen of the candles to be priced, time myself, multiply the hours by $3, divide by 12, and come up with the price per candle that I must have to make my hourly wage.

As you become more experienced with candles, you will be able to quite accurately determine what price the market will allow. Bigger candles sell for money, right? But they cost you very little more in materials, and perhaps they require only as much time to make as a small candle. You can either raise your wages per hour, or leave them at $3 (for example) and plan on providing a bargain for your buyers.

When I developed the candle I call Charisma, which weighs 9½ pounds, and is 6½ x 6½ x 6½ inches, I figured I could make the candle for $4.50 wholesale and still make my $3 per hour. This made the retail price only $9, a tremendous bargain considering the size and weight of the candle.

By keeping the price low, I sold over 300 of them to one store, and they were able to pass on a unique candle at a bargain price to their customers. Everyone was happy.

You will undoubtedly develop some very beautiful candles that you won't be able to sell for half the retail price because of the time involved to make them. Hold on to them until you go to a craft show.

Because you must call your candles *something* to differentiate them, you may as well name them something that might help them sell. There seems to be a great preoccupation with the occult and mysterious in this country right now, and people like such names as *Witchery, Charisma,* and *Magic.* Or you might try the signs of the zodiac, which are also popular now.

I make one candle with a different African mask on each of the four sides, and I call it *Witch Doctor's Family Portrait.* Some people find that amusing, and one of my dealers says the name has helped her sell a number of them.

Be sure that the name is carried on every candle. If you don't wish to have labels printed, construct a rubber stamp and put the name on the self-sticking labels you can buy in almost any stationery store.

I have shared with you the four candles which have been most successful for me, but I haven't even scratched the surface of the many kinds of candles it is possible to make. There are sand-cast candles, hand-carved candles, hand-painted candles, sculptured wax candles, crushed-ice candles, cut-glass candles, container candles, and candles made in plastic bags, to name a few. There are numerous books on the market, and in your library, which will teach you how to make these and many, many other kinds of candles. Further reading will broaden your horizons greatly, and you may want to try your hand at some of the other kinds of candles. The more you experiment and work with candles, the more likely you will be to come up with new and different candle ideas. Let your imagination run free, it could make you a bundle.

4

Marketing Your Candles

Now you are ready to begin marketing your candles.

There are several ways of making money at this time. One sure way is a hobby and craft or art and craft show. These are fairs where artists and craftsmen bring their wares to show and to sell.

Some cities have an artists' equity which will keep you posted on when and where the shows are to be. Some shows are sponsored by merchants in a shopping center, some are put on by individuals who are paid a percentage or a flat fee for doing the show, some are church or school bazaars at which you may buy space.

The more shows you participate in, the more shows you will be invited into later. Many of the people who exhibit in these shows do it for a living, and they'll tell you how and where to find them (provided, of course, they don't make candles!)

Usually the shows are on weekends, and you will buy a space for $7–$20. In some shows, you will be expected to pay for space *and* give a percentage of what you sell, but this happens only occasionally.

Call your local newspaper for information on arts and crafts organizations who may be having shows, and check with the managers of shopping centers near you. Watch your paper for bazaars and flea markets.

When you find a show that sounds interesting, contact the promoter and arrange to become a part of it. Be sure to ascertain if crafts are allowed, as many shows exclude all but original art work.

If the show is juried, this simply means that a judge or a panel of judges will have to see your work and decide if it meets the standards for the show before you are accepted. Don't let it bother you, but do be sure your workmanship is the best of which you are capable.

Examples of decorative candles.

When your application has been accepted, you should do two things. First, if there is a retail sales tax in your state, write your state tax office and secure a retail tax number.

When you get to the point that you need a wholesale tax number (later), you will pay no state tax on your materials because they will be resold and the consumer will ultimately pay the tax. Now the consumer will be buying the candle directly from you, and you will be responsible for collecting the state's tax and getting it to the tax office.

The second thing that you should do to prepare for the craft show is to make the candles—lots of them. It seems to be better to have a few of many styles rather than a lot of only two or three styles. This gives people a wide choice which they seem to like. Also, it will give you a chance to see which styles sell best in your area.

You will probably be allocated eight to ten feet of space in which to show. Plan to decorate it as attractively as possible, with colors that are appropriate to the season. Also be sure you have plenty of change before you arrive, and try to have a cash box to keep it in, preferably one that locks.

It is nice to have someone to help you run the booth. That will not only give each of you a rest break to eat and see the rest of the show, but it also will help you keep a close eye on your candles to see that no one damages or steals them. One day I had a gentleman try to pull the top off of a *Magic* candle to see how it was made, and little ones love to dig their fingernails into shiny wax candles.

There really is no way of knowing in advance whether a show will make you money or not, but one good indicator is the amount of publicity given the show. The more advertising there is, the more people are likely to turn out and the more you'll probably make.

It's a pretty indefinite situation, but I know of at least two people who make their living going to craft shows, so it can't be too bad. I, myself, have grossed as much as $200 in a weekend at a show.

If you find showing too strenuous, and it does take stamina, try selling your candles through a boutique or small gift shop. If you live in a sparsely populated area, you may not have much choice about which shop to choose, but if you are in a large, metropolitan area, you should be discriminating about the shop you choose.

First of all, is it in a location where there are many people who can afford to spend money on candles? Even some of the seemingly affluent suburbanites have kids' teeth to straighten and cars to pay for, and there's little left for luxury items. Choose a shop in a solid community, preferably with a median income of $12–$15,000 per year.

Then ask yourself if the shop is in an area where it gets lots of foot traffic. If it's part of a small community center or downtown in a suburb or small town, there will be many people walking by it. That often brings in customers who might pass right by a more isolated shop.

When you think you have found a suitable shop, go in and see the merchandise offered. If they do not sell candles, they are probably not going to be interested in buying your things, and you are not yet ready to supply them with a whole candle department. If they do have candles, notice how they are displayed.

I sold to a large store in a tourist area near my home, and I thought surely it would be a good market, but the store was so crammed full of gifts, candles, and novelties that there wasn't room to display the candles well, and they didn't sell at all.

If the store does carry candles, but no decorative ones, you are probably not going to do much business there either.

Keep these things in mind, and when you have selected a shop, get the name of the owner or the buyer, and call him for an appointment.

When you meet your buyer, introduce yourself and show him your candles. Do be friendly, but try not to take your buyer's time with unrelated subjects, as they are usually very busy people and have many other things to do than just chat.

You may be asked if you will sell your candles on consignment. This means that you take your candles to the shop, but you aren't paid for them until and unless they sell.

I have never placed any candles out on consignment, because I always felt that a store takes better care of things they have invested their money in. Nor did I care to stock someone's shelves for them at my expense. If you do place your candles out on consignment, you should expect to get at least some of them back pretty "shopworn" and battered.

The shop which takes your candles on consignment should not expect to keep 50% of the retail price. The usual percentage for consignment sales is 25%–33%. This should be thoroughly understood before any deliveries are made.

I have given you instructions for making several of the candles which have sold well for me, and I have given you a couple of ideas on how to make money with your candles.

There are literally hundreds of other types of candles that you can make, and many excellent books available on how to make them. I recommend that you read as many of them as possible and experiment with making many different kinds to broaden your perspectives and give you ideas for further candlecrafting.

One more suggestion about the type of candle you decide to sell. It isn't profitable to try to compete with the big companies with plain candles or tapers. They can operate on a much smaller margin than you could hope to, and they can provide hundreds and thousands of candles in a huge variety of colors and sizes that you could never hope to do profitably on a small scale. I think you'll find that your best bet is in decorative or novelty candles.

5
The Roaster Oven Stage

Probably very soon after you begin marketing your candles, you will outgrow the Double Boiler Stage of candlemaking and be ready to move on to the Roaster Oven Stage. In order to do this, you will need some additional materials.

First of all you must write your state tax office for a resale or wholesale tax number because you will be buying in quantity. In most states, when a consumer purchases a product at retail price, he must pay a sales tax of a given percentage to the state. This is collected by the retailer and paid back to the state periodically, as you already know from attending craft shows. If, however, you are buying a product which you plan to resell, you should not pay a tax on this item. Nor do you pay a tax on the things which go into your product (e.g. wax, wick, dyes, boxes, etc.). Your buyers will not pay a tax to you either, because the tax is paid only once, by the consumer or user of the product. So, in order not to pay tax on an item used to make your candles, get a wholesale tax number, and give it to your suppliers when you place an order with them.

The next thing you will need to start the Roaster Oven Stage is work area. This can be a basement, utility room, garage, or any place that you have electricity and running water.

Finally, of course, you will need a roaster oven. These are the thermostatically controlled electric ovens which have a removable liner. They sell for about $40 new, but if you'll go to a few garage sales, or watch the local classified ads, you're bound to find a second-hand one for half price or less.

To use the roaster oven as a melting pot, break up about 20 pounds of wax, so that it will fit into the vat. Put the lid on, and set the thermostat between 250–300°. It will take an hour or so before that much wax is ready to pour.

Some other items which you will need in the Roaster Oven Stage are:

1. *Labels* Your candles will look much more professional when each is attractively labeled with your company name. Labels can cost as much as $1 apiece, and since you'll need the self-sticking kind, you can hardly hope to have them made and imprinted for less than 8-10¢ apiece, a large outlay, especially if it's on a small candle. I solved this problem by ordering 250 gold address labels for $1.98 (and postage) from Walter Drake and Co., Drake Building, Colorado Springs, Colorado. They are gold foil with a black decorative border, self-sticking, and they can be imprinted with several lines of words. I have two kinds. One simply says, A Deannie Candle, and I use it as a box label. The other reads, "A Deannie Candle, Handmade and Decorated" and it is affixed to every candle I sell.

2. *Business cards* The more professional you appear, the easier it will be to sell your candles. You can have 1,000 cards printed up for $8–$10. Be sure to include your company name, your name, address and phone number. You may wish to use a little slogan or "buy-line." I had "Quality With A Flair" imprinted right under Deannie Candles on my cards, and an artist's palette and brushes put up in one corner. These cards are nice to use when calling on a buyer, and they're almost a necessity at trade shows.

3. *Stationery* Stationery will cost you more than cards, about $12 for 1,000 photo-printed sheets, but it is a great help to have, and if you must choose between cards and stationery, pick stationery.

Use it whenever you make or answer any inquiries concerning your business, or when ordering supplies. You may also want to prepare your bills on it.

Remember, your stationery goes when you can't. Choose some that will reflect your good taste and make a good impression wherever it goes.

4. *Order book* These are available through office supply houses, and almost a necessity to keep your orders and your bookkeeping straight. Number each order and don't start with "1" unless you want all of your early buyers to know you're a rank beginner. I suggest that the number one be prefixed with the year or any whole number (e.g. 721, 722, or 201, etc.).

Take your order book with you, and write out the order as you take it from your buyer. List each candle name or number ordered, how many, what colors, unit price (i.e. how much apiece), the date the order is taken, the address of the store, where the order is to be delivered, and when. You may wish to have both your signature and the signature of the buyer on the order, but it isn't really necessary. Large stores have their own purchase orders, which they fill out and give to you, but I suspect that you won't need to worry about that when you first begin the Roaster Oven Stage.

There will probably be a place on the order blank marked "terms." That means if you offer any discounts for prompt payment or charge any penalties for late payment, you should so indicate.

In my business, I like to have my money right away. I have purchased supplies and equipment, produced what I promised to produce, and since I'm not in the business of loaning money, I want my money when I deliver my merchandise.

To encourage prompt payment, and to save me the bother of billing, etc., I offer a 2% discount for cash on delivery. Second best is payment within a few days, so I allow a 1% discount for payment in 10 days or less.

Let's suppose that I deliver an order totaling $100 and my buyer pays me when I deliver. I will deduct 2%, or $2 from what he owes me. If he waits 10 days, he only gets $1 off.

I offer no discounts for orders paid for from 10–30 days after delivery, and after 30 days, I start charging my accounts a service charge of 1½% per month for using my money. This amounts to 18% a year, quite a bit more interest than a sound business has to pay for money, and it is usually enough to deter the late payers.

Despite discounts and penalties, you will undoubtedly run into someone who stocks your candles and doesn't want to pay for them. All I can suggest, is that you keep dunning them, including the service charge when applicable. If they refuse to pay, you may have to take them to small claims court or mention the problem to the Better Business Bureau. As soon as you get your money, drop that account! As a solo businessman, you haven't the time or the energy to do a lot of unnecessary billing and collecting.

Give your buyer a copy of the order he has placed, and keep one or two for yourself. Try to put your company name, address, and phone number on your buyer's copy, so that he can locate you if he needs to.

While you are making up the order, it may help you to post the order in your work area and check the items off as they are finished. Then, when the order is complete, double-check to see that the colors and quantities of candles ordered have been made.

Your order book will also help you at tax time because you will have a careful list of what you have sold all year in one handy place.

Then too, you may need to refer back to the previous year's books for buyer's information. One of my shops places nearly exactly the same Christmas order with me each year. The owner just says, "Make the same order as last year, and add. . . ." whatever new candles he wishes to buy.

And, on occasion, a buyer may ask you how many of a certain type of candle he ordered within a given time the year or two before. If you have a well-kept order book, you can tell him instantly.

5. *Packaging or boxes* To me, this is but a necessary evil. First of all, boxes cost money. The smallest and cheapest one I use costs 8.5¢, and that's only if I order 1,000 or more. The price is higher for less boxes. And the more expensive and bigger ones cost 25¢ to $1 each.

Secondly, they take either time or space. If they come folded down, they must be assembled, and this takes time, and time is money in any business. If they come set up or preassembled, they gobble up floor space, collect dust, and cost even more money because you've paid somebody else to do this.

Finally, they do contribute to pollution because they have to be dealt with when they are discarded.

As far as I'm concerned, boxes are evil, but as I said, they are necessary, and they even have some good points. First of all they protect your product from dust or marring.

Secondly they allow your buyers to stock your candles in an orderly fashion. Can you imagine a stockroom or warehouse full of grocery bags filled with tissue-wrapped candles?

Thirdly, a retail buyer nearly always wants a box for his candle—so he can give it as a gift or just to get it home without hurting it, or so that he can store it at home or send it through the mail.

Finally, a box can advertise for you. As long as you have to have them, you may as well emblazon them with your company name so that everyone can see whose candle that customer chose!

If you live in or near a reasonably large city, you should have no trouble packaging your candles. How fancy you get is up to you.

I personally prefer to package my candles in corrugated cardboard boxes. I usually wrap the candle in tissue paper first, and then box it.

Brown corrugated boxes may not be very pretty, but they are cheaper than gift boxes, and infinitely more sturdy. Besides, all the candles I make will fit into stock boxes! Every company has standard sizes that they carry in stock. These are cheaper and faster to get than custom-made boxes.

I keep 4x4x4-inch boxes for Fleurettes and Rosettes; 5x5x5-inch boxes for Spheres; 6x6x6-inch boxes for Magic; and 8x8x8-inch boxes for Medallion and larger. And when I graduated to the Big Pot stage, I even bought big boxes in which to pack and deliver these little boxes.

These are nice, but not a necessity unless, of course, you are going to ship your candles out of town. Then you will need large boxes which exactly hold several candles (individually boxed, of course).

6. *Product liability insurance* Nearly every manufacturer carries this insurance. It is, simply stated, your protection against a consumer who might get hurt or suffer damages from using your product.

Let us suppose that someone's house burns down, and they say your candle caused the fire because it didn't function properly. Or some child ate one of your candles and became ill or died. If you have product liability insurance, your insurance company will handle any lawsuits or procedures which might result from such an occurrence.

Such policies have flexible limits of liability, depending on how much of a premium you are prepared to pay. But most people will tell you it's a good idea to have too much protection, rather than too little. The amount of insurance can be determined by you or if you're dealing with a large store, they may insist on certain limits of liability.

If you have a homeowner's or fire insurance policy with a company you like, it would probably be well to start there inquiring about product liability insurance. If you do not have an insurance company, or if yours declines to insure you (your business is very small, remember, and hardly worth anyone's trouble), then I suggest that you start down the yellow pages until you find someone who will carry you.

For $75 a year, I have hundreds of thousands of dollars of protection. This, though I never plan to need it, seems fair enough.

7. *A way of showing your candles* By the time you are in the Roaster Oven Stage of candlemaking, you will no doubt have developed many different styles or types of candles that you want to sell. If you have small enough or few enough samples, you may wish to carry one of each in to show your buyer. Then I recommend that you make some kind of a candle cart.

When I show samples, I pack them into a folding grocery cart which has a perky, polka-dotted, plastic liner. Although this isn't easy to get in and out of the car, it's much easier than having to carry a big box of candles by hand. If you have a flair for the unusual and don't mind a few strange looks, you could paint and decorate a child's wagon for the job. It might even be fun!

If you have too many candle styles to carry, then I suggest that you get pictures taken of each candle. If you have a good camera and a knack for such things, you can probably take the pictures yourself. If not, you will have to hire a photographer.

The man who photographed my candles, came out to the house, set up a drape, and took several shots of each candle. I selected the one which best showed each candle and made myself something of a catalog.

I bought a picture album and placed each candle on its own page.

Examples of decorative candles.

Then I typed the name, dimensions, colors, and price of the candle and told whether it was sold in bulk or individually boxed, and what type of box was used (i.e. mailer, brown corrugated or gift box) and placed these specifications right under the picture.

Besides saving wear and tear on me and saving wear and tear on the candle samples, this made a handy catalog when we started getting out-of-town buyers. I just sent them my catalog and a stamped, addressed container for them to return it in.

Even if you have a set of candle pictures, you should take at least one sample candle with you to show a prospective buyer. It will give him an idea of your workmanship.

Although it will cost you a little bit extra to set up for large-scale candlemaking, you are giving yourself a raise because now you are ready to start buying some of your materials in large, or should I say larger, quantities. There's no need, for example, to continue to pay 25¢ per pound for wax, when you can buy it for 13.5¢/lb. or maybe even less.

Look in the yellow pages of your phone book under wax. Or call the oil companies such as Standard, Gulf, Mobil, etc., and ask their prices, minimum orders, and delivery charges, if any, on paraffin(s) with the melting points, etc., that you need.

Don't be surprised if the dealer doesn't seem too happy to have you as a paraffin customer. He only makes a few pennies on each *case* of wax he brings you, and he has to load and unload those 50 or 60-pound boxes several times. Keep this in mind when you order, and buy as much as you can at one time.

At this point you will find yourself eligible for 25–50% discounts from the mold and candlemaking supply houses. They carry everything you can possibly need for candlemaking, and by ordering large enough quantities, you can save a large percent of the retail price.

Write to each of the companies in the List of Suppliers, and any others you may know of, and ask for a statement of their dealer terms. If they allow it, you may want to place a small retail order first, to acquaint yourself with the quality of the materials involved. You will be very disappointed if you order several hundred dollars worth of molds and other supplies and then find they aren't sturdy enough to stand up to the daily use you will give them.

When you have found the company which best satisfies your needs for molds, wicking, dyes, etc., then order enough of everything you need to qualify for discounts and maybe even freight allowances. Besides saving you dollars on purchases, ordering in quantity will save you time and the effort of running to get bits and pieces of things.

Try to order as many of your supplies as possible from one source.

For example, one company that can sell you molds, wicking, dye, trims, and accessories is more valuable to you than ordering piecemeal from several places.

"Now," you ask, "what shall I buy?"

You have no doubt developed several candles which you wish to produce in quantity for sale. Decide which molds, wicking, dyes, etc., you need to make a large quantity of them, and order these and materials for any other candle styles at one time.

For example, let's suppose you want to make Fleurettes, a dozen or two at a time. You would want to order 12–24 three-inch square molds, 100 yards of wicking, enough dye to color several hundred pounds of wax, and antiquing glaze plus five plastic molds for every one metal mold you pour. If you have other candle styles, you will want to order molds, etc., for them as well. When you have all the equipage for the Roaster Oven Stage, and you are ready to pour multiple candles, you will have to change your pouring and manufacturing methods somewhat. You will need several places to cool candles now instead of just one or two. A deep sink or a long metal trough will do nicely. Also, you will probably want to make large, shallow boxes of sand in which to cool the wax embellishments.

From now on, you'll find that you won't be doing much sitting around in your candle shop. Consider the steps in making just one candle:

1. melt wax
2. tie mold
3. pour
4. cool
5. remove from water bath and chill
6. remove from mold
7. fill and level
8. assemble
9. finish (antique or highlight)
10. label and package

It is improbable that you will complete a batch of candles in one day. Rather, you will probably have only partially finished them. There will always be something else for you to work on while you wait for wax to melt or cool, or paint to dry, etc.

But the nicest thing of all is that you can stop and start anytime and any way you like. With the exception of pouring when the wax is just the right temperature, there is no step in the candlemaking process that you can't abandon instantly, if you so desire. Even the pouring can be delayed, if you don't mind reheating the wax.

Should you make only enough candles to fill orders you have on hand, or should you "stock," that is make several extra candles of each style and color to have on hand when the next order comes in? This will depend largely on how much time and space you have. If you have time left after filling orders, and if you have space to store finished candles where they will not get dusty or too hot or cold, etc., you will probably want to stock.

I have done it both ways, and much prefer to keep stock. Then when an order comes in, I don't have to drop everything else in my life to fill it. Many times when I've had candles in stock, I've had to make only ten or twelve more candles to completely fill an order.

Another consideration about stocking is, can you fill your orders promptly enough if you don't stock? I usually tell my buyers it will take three weeks to deliver their order, and then I work like a Turk to fill it sooner. I really feel that waiting longer than that is too much to ask of a store.

But if you get an order for several hundred candles, it may not be possbile for you to fill it quickly unless you have some in reserve. You will learn from experience about how many to make ahead, as you will see that your stores usually order "x" number of "y" style in "z" colors, and you can work from that.

Now that you are geared up to make candles by the dozen, you'll probably be looking for greener pastures in the form of larger-sized stores or shops which sell greater volumes of candles.

How do you sell to a larger store?

Timing is very important in selling. The largest volume of candles sold is from September through December, when some 50% of the year's volume moves out. Buyers for large stores usually begin purchasing for this time in May or June, and their Christmas buying is nearly always complete by July. Smaller stores don't need such a long, advance time, but if you wait until September, smaller stores will already have been to the big gift shows, etc., and they may have already spent all of their budget.

If at all possible, start in late spring with all of your kinds of candles, Christmas and otherwise. If you can't do that, the period right after Christmas usually finds the shelves and stockrooms cleaned out and badly in need of stock.

Some merchants won't order until after inventory because they have to pay a tax on their stock, but others like to have a good selection on their shelves right *after* Christmas for all the people who get money for gifts. People do shop in great numbers during this time to take advantage of the sales. If you can have your candles ready to deliver right away, you may make a few sales during this after-the-holidays period.

When you make your call to your buyer, you should make every effort to be businesslike and not appear to be a hobbyist trying to make a few dollars on the side. The buyers in the larger stores tell me that *every*one who makes *any*thing comes trying to sell to them, and they spend hundreds of valuable hours trying to dodge or ease out of their offices away from hoardes of junior achievers, boy scouts, housewives, women's clubs, etc., who want them to buy their handmade items.

So when you call for an appointment, first find out the name of the buyer for the decorative candles. Then you might say something like this:

"Mr. Jones, this is Eugenia Bourn with Deannie Candles in Chicago. We have some [or a line of] lovely decorative candles that I would like to show you if you have time."

He may say that he's overstocked now and doesn't need any, or he may indicate an interest in seeing them.

If he does want to see your candles, you might say, "What day is a good one for you, and what time?"

You should already know *your* schedule, so that if he wants to see you on a day that you can't make it, you can say so right then without having to call him back later to juggle the appointment times. When you have agreed on a date, time and place, thank him and say good-by.

When the appointed time arrives, present your card by way of introduction, exchange pleasantries if your buyer seems to have time, and then get right back to work. Have everything ready. Know your candles and their prices, and be able to answer any questions about every style.

If you have a book with pictures, fine. If not, show all of your candles before expecting him to order.

If he does order, write each item, color, quantity, etc., down in your order book—yes, even if he gives you a purchase order. That way you'll have a record and handy reference for use during and after filling the order. You may want to type up a price list for him and leave it for future reference. Thank him for his order and leave.

When the store's order is finished, and ready to deliver, you may find the following hints helpful for delivery. If the store is a large one, and you have gotten a purchase order, it may have instructions on it as to date and place of delivery, bills of lading, packing slips, and invoices. If you do not have such instructions, you should find out when and where your buyer wants the candles delivered. Call him to find out, if necessary.

Package the candles so that one man can handle them, or, if you will do the delivering, so that you can load and unload them by yourself.

You will be expected to load the candles out of their conveyance and on to the loading dock.

Make a packing slip to accompany the order. This is simply a list which tells the number and contents of the packages in the shipment. This slip, as well as any other pieces of correspondence concerning the order, should contain the name and address of the store, your company name and address, department number (if any) and order number (both yours and the store's).

You will also want to include an invoice when you deliver the order. This is a bill, and it should contain an itemized list of the complete order with unit price and total price for each style of candle, as well as a grand total. Terms should also be noted on this paper, and, of course, your address, order numbers, and so forth.

Place the packing slip and invoices in an envelope, and tape them on the outside of one carton. Label this envelope and carton, or it may be overlooked. Or, you may put the envelope inside one package and mark the package so that the stock room will know that it is there.

Remember, the candles will be labeled with their price as they are placed in the stock room, so the people there must know the price of each article. Even if it's a small store and manned by its owner, he will appreciate having prices handy, so he doesn't have to go digging for them.

If it's a small store, and you are expecting cash on delivery, you should time the delivery so that you'll arrive when someone who has the authority can pay you. Otherwise, any time during delivery hours is fine.

You will probably go to the delivery entrance rather than through the front door, as you did when you were selling. You will be expected to place the candles on the dock of the store. Don't expect help unloading, and if you get it, you really should tip whoever helps you, unless it is the owner himself.

Usually the invoice you bring with the candles is forwarded to accounts payable (or goes to the person who pays the bills), but if you want to make sure they get the bill, you may send a copy—be sure it's marked DUPLICATE—to the office.

If you offer a discount, you may get payment right away. Otherwise, expect a full 30 days or more to elapse before you receive your payment. When you get your money, do yourself the favor of writing it down in your account books.

Sooner or later, the day will come when you will have to have an accounting, and it will be much less difficult for you if you have some kind of accurate records to go by.

When I was in this stage, I had a daily calendar notebook which had a balance sheet for each month and for the year at the end of the book. When I got a check or made money at a show, I put it down with the date under the appropriate month. As I spent money for wax and supplies, I noted it and saved the receipts and cancelled checks in an envelope thrust between the pages representing that month. I totaled each month with debits and credits, and then entered them on the yearly balance sheet. When income tax time rolled around, I had only to thumb back through my records to take deductions and figure my profits. If you can't find a notebook such as this, you might want to make your own looseleaf type. A sample sheet might look something like this:

JANUARY

Date	Item	Debit	Credit
12	Wax (ck#310 Standard Oil)	$67.75	
15	The Candle Shop (ck#511—order#756)		173.00
16	Dye and supplies (ck#311 Handymakers)	12.50	
17	Cleaning service (ck#312 Cleansweep)	15.00	
18	Utilities (ck#313 gas 33% of bill	5.15	
	ck#314 elec.)	6.12	
23	Lighter Side Gifts (order#5310—ck#398)	46.52	225.00
			398.00

Receipts and cancelled checks can be kept in envelopes, stapled together to the sheet, or placed in a pocket of the notebook.

Incidentally, if you'll notice, I entered 33% of the utility bills. Approximately one-third of my house is given over to the candle operation, and I am therefore entitled to deduct one-third of depreciation on the house, utilities, etc., on the income tax. The same is true for the use of the telephone. Do consult your tax bureau or an attorney about your deductions.

After delivering your candles, wait ten days to two weeks, and then call your buyer and see that the order was satisfactory. He probably won't be out of anything, but you can ask if he needs any more and when he wants you to check back with him again. Make a note on your calendar to call him back whenever he says.

No matter how careful you are, you will undoubtedly have a broken candle or a dissatisfied customer somewhere along the way. My policy has always been to replace immediately any candle which failed to function satisfactorily for a customer. The shop will usually split the cost with you, but even if they don't, you have a reputation to uphold, and you want it to be one of quality and satisfaction. Take the loss, if necessary. There will be very few instances.

It has also been my policy to repair, whenever possible, or to replace candles which get marred or broken badly enough that they won't sell.

Besides the fact that this is above and beyond the call of duty, it isn't always possible, but it certainly keeps your stores happy, and it isn't really much skin off your nose. Everyone appreciates someone who goes out of his way for them.

Speaking of reputations and being known, any publicity you can get about your candles will be helpful to you.

About the end of my first year in the candle business, a reporter came into one of the shops that carried my candles and asked the proprietor (my buyer) if there was a candle factory in the area, because she wanted to do a feature on it. He told her about me, and I got a very nice write-up with a picture in the Chicago *Daily News.*

Then a few weeks later, a lady who goes to my church, and who does free-lance reporting, asked me if she could do a feature on me for our local Arlington Heights paper. By this time I was even shipping a few candles out of state, and her headline on a very flattering article about me was "Deannie Candles Glow Even in Boston."

I got a few orders I never would have gotten without the articles, and several months after that these local articles helped me get a write up in the *Ladies Home Journal.*

The Journal was running a series about *How to Earn Money in Your Spare Time,* and they were looking for unusual ways that people did so. I sent them the clippings on me, told them a little bit about myself, and pretty soon a staff writer called to interview me long distance for the *Journal* article.

I firmly believe that these little releases opened some doors for me. I was just lucky, of course. I just happened to be in the right place, in the right business, at the right time, but you, too, will be of interest to many people, and if you could be the subject of a feature article in your local paper or get a write up in a periodical, you'll find it helps sell you and your candles. Many clubs and fraternal organizations have newsletters or even nationally distributed publications about their members. Let them know you are around, and available for interviewing.

Besides helping your sales, publicity will undoubtedly attract a number of individuals or groups who would like for you to teach them how to make candles. Teaching candle making is easily done at this stage, and it is a good way of earning money.

Many park districts or recreation departments, and even night schools, offer courses in arts and crafts, and with the mushrooming interest in candlemaking, most of them also offer courses in this. If they don't, they should. Go offer your services as the teacher or you may want to offer a course in your home. Just be sure such a course doesn't interfere with your neighbors or become a nuisance in any way.

There are so many types of candles to use as topics that you could probably teach the crafting of a different candle every week for a year and still not have made a major dent in the possibilities. But probably you will offer a semester course with perhaps 20 lessons at a maximum. It will take considerable planning and preparation for this endeavor, but once the curriculum is established and materials are purchased, the rest of it is easier.

Your part as teacher will be demonstration and evaluation. Your students will watch you make each type of candle. Then each student will go home and execute one of his own. You will evaluate it when it is finished, and tell him how to correct any mistakes.

To suggest a few types of candles you may want to teach, I have prepared a sample outline for a candlemaking course:

I. Familiarization. Tell your students what equipment and supplies they will need, and where they can purchase these.

II. Demonstrate a basic candle. This will show wicking, sealing, pouring, cooling, and leveling. Point out things to watch during pouring, such as proper temperatures, oil content of wax, cooling temperatures, care of molds, and so forth. Then when your students bring in their work, if there is a problem, be sure to call it to the attention of the class, tell its cause and how to prevent it from happening again.

III. Pour a hurricane or votive type candle. As you go along, be sure to carefully explain everything you do and anticipate any trouble areas for your students.

IV. Demonstrate the making of a latex mold from a figurine or a piece of suitable shaped cut glass, etc. Pour a candle in a latex mold. Demonstrate wicking a cooled candle.

V. Prepare sand and pour a sand-cast candle.

VI. Pour a candle with foil, plastic flowers or ferns embedded in it.

VII. Demonstrate a candle made in a one-time glass mold (e.g. fruit molds, balls o' fire).

VIII. Demonstrate an appliqued candle (i.e. one that is poured in separate pieces and assembled, such as *Magic*).

IX. Show how to whip wax and demonstrate ways of decorating candles with it.

X. Teach candle dipping.

XI. Make an ice candle for the class.

XII. Show how to make a hand-molded candle (e.g. ropes and whimseys).

XIII. Explain sculpturing wax and demonstrate how to make flowers, fruit, etc., out of wax and how to apply them to a basic candle.

XIV. Make some floating candles.

XV. Explain the proper use of scents and pour some scented candles.

XVI Paint with oils on a candle.

XVII. Show how to carve a candle to decorate it. Also show ways to distress the finish.

XVIII. Apply tissue paper, braid, glitter decals, etc., as trims for candles.

XIX. Paint a candle with hot wax.

These are but a few of the possible lessons you might teach in a candlemaking course.

To give you an idea of how one lesson might go, let us take XVI and elaborate on its presentation.

Before class begins, you will need to have all your materials assembled. You will need:

1. A finished basic candle in a shape that lends itself to a design, such as a round, oval or square.
2. A design which fits the candle to be decorated.
3. Tracing paper.
4. Masking tape.
5. Dull pencil.
6. Brushes.
7. Artist's oil paints.

First, draw your design. It should be in proportion to the size of the candle, and it should follow the rules of composition. Then transfer the design to tracing paper (Fig. 39).

Tape the tracing paper over the candle with the design in the place you want it (Fig. 40), and go over the outline of the design with a soft, dull, pencil (Fig. 41). This will leave a tiny line in the wax which will help you keep your design under control.

Remove the tracing paper, and paint the candle (Fig. 42). Since this is an original work of art, you may feel free to sign it just as an artist does.

Because this progress may not take the entire class period, you may wish also to spray paint a candle through a stencil you have prepared or through a paper doily.

Simply tape the design or doily securely in place and spray with a can of spray paint. Then peel off paper, and you'll have a lovely design on the candle.

If you are planning to sell supplies to your students, you will make more money than just the lesson, and you will be able to save your students money too.

That is because you will buy in quantity and thus be eligible for a

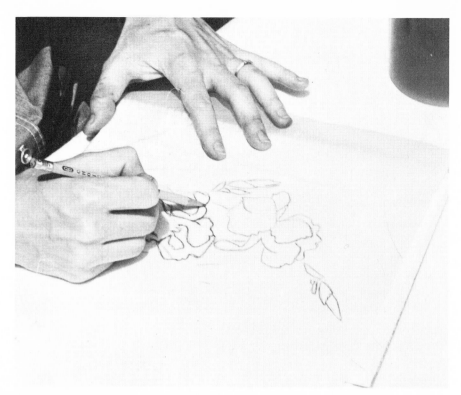

FIG. 39 *Draw your design and transfer it to tracing paper*

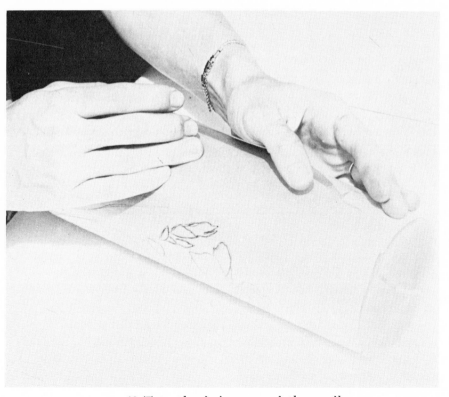

FIG. 40 *Tape the design around the candle*

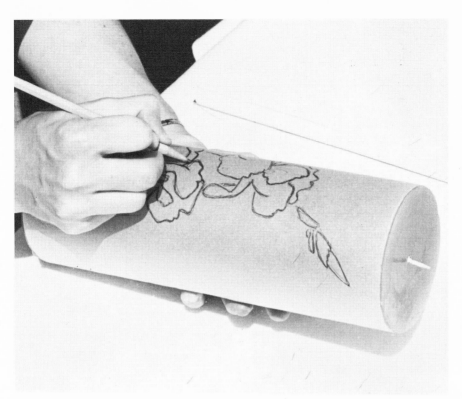

FIG. 41 *Transfer the outline of the design to the candle*

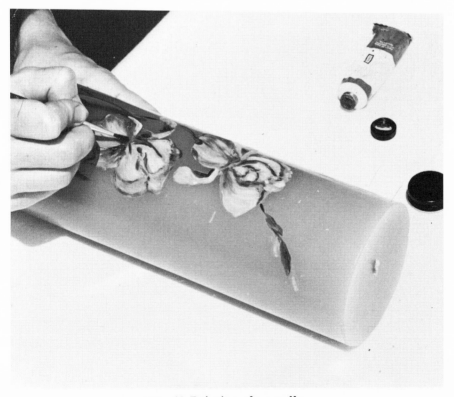

FIG. 42 *Painting the candle*

40–50% discount on retail prices. You can sell the supplies to your students at 20–25% over cost, keep some for your trouble, and save them 25–30% on their supplies.

This method also assures them of having the supplies when they need them.

If you do not want to bother supplying your students, be sure you notify the hobby stores where they will probably trade so that they will have enough stock to allow them to make the candles you demonstrate.

6

The Big Pot Stage

By now, you are probably becoming well established in your business, and you are ready to move on to bigger and more profitable ventures. And so it is that we arrive at the Big Pot Stage.

There are several additional things that you will need to carry on business at this level. First on the list should be an inexhaustible supply of headache remedies. Somehow there seems always to be a new problem to be faced—you're out of only one kind of box, or your supplies to fill a large seasonal order didn't arrive because of some strike somewhere, or the buyer for your biggest account seems to be ignoring you, or the store you sold to in some distant state took a discount when they didn't rate it, or the income tax has to be done right at the time you're making up the biggest order you ever got. And so it may go. But to help you put up with the petty annoyances, keep thinking of all the people who have to punch a time clock, or hire, train, and supervise several employees, or commute half a day to their job, or make huge payments on fancy new equipment.

The one article you cannot do without in this stage is, of course, a big pot. When I first needed to pour more than 100 pounds of wax a day, it was suggested that I look around for a used coffee urn, the type used in hotels and restaurants. These might work satisfactorily for you, but you should watch for two things. First of all, they usually have neoprene gaskets that quickly disintegrate when exposed to hot wax. This may be overcome by the use of a ball-cock gasket. Secondly these urns are usually steam heated, and the presence of water in the wax is a distinct possibility.

It was also suggested to me that the wax be melted directly over a stove burner in a large cooking pot such as those used by hotels or institutions. Or, if you could find a used one, a water-jacketed steam kettle is suitable. These cost more than $1,000 new, and they seldom wear out, but occasionally they are available, and the man I talked to said that the large cosmetic companies make their lipsticks in them, so they should be suitable for wax.

You may have to do some innovative thinking to get your big pot, or you may wish to use the solution I found. I managed to find a huge, stainless steel vat, whose original function is still obscure. It came attached to 3 legs about 14 inches off the floor. Under this, I had a gas burner mounted (i.e. the type found in hot water heaters) and at the bottom of the vat, I had a ball-cock spigot installed (i.e. the type used on some coffee urns).

Wax is then placed in the pot and the flame underneath turned on low until enough wax is melted. Then the wax is colored according to whatever formula I need for a specific color. I open the spigot and draw off whatever amount is needed, either directly into my metal molds or into a metal pouring pitcher and then into plastic or other molds. It may be rather primitive, and it certainly looks a little less than professional, but it gets the job done very efficiently.

One word of caution here. Never, *never* leave this type of pot unattended for one minute. Until the wax has covered the bottom of the pot, it will smoke, and you must stir it constantly to keep cooler wax circulating over the flame. Once you have acquired a pretty good little puddle of wax, you may go on and do something else, but do not leave the room or get involved on the telephone or answer the door or something and leave this wax heating. It only takes a second to turn off the gas. Turn the burner *off*, and don't light it again until you can stay with it.

Next on the list of supplies for the Big Pot Stage is plenty of wax. You'll be surprised how very quickly 50 cases disappear when you are melting a couple hundred pounds at a time.

Of course 50–100 cases of paraffin are going to require some storage space, but at least it can be almost anywhere. I keep 50 cases in my garage, and 25 to 50 in my basement. If you become desperate for space, you can always plop a 4x8 sheet of plywood down on 30 or 40 cases stacked about five high and make a work table.

Another thing that may set you back a bit is the bill for 100 cases of wax. At 13–14¢ per pound for 5,000 or 6,000 pounds of wax, you're talking about $700–800. To make the best use of your money, I recommend that you establish a commercial account with your chosen wax dealer so that you may get 30 days or more to pay for wax purchased. By buying at the right time, you can make and sell enough candles in 30 days to pay for the paraffin, and have plenty of wax left over for future orders.

Or, if you prefer, you can probably get a 1–2% discount for cash on delivery.

Another thing you should look into at this stage is aniline candle dyes. Look in the yellow pages of any metropolitan phone book for the numbers of the large chemical companies. Call them and tell them you want to buy aniline candle dyes in fairly small quantities. They probably will require a much larger order than you intended to place, but they will direct you to smaller companies that will be glad to handle your order.

Once you get the names of several, either write or call them and tell them what color dyes and in what quantities you want them. They will undoubtedly send you samples, which you should try as soon as possible. When you can, order all your dyes at one time from one company. Use their suggested proportions of dye to paraffin until you can work out your own formulas for the colors you desire.

In addition to securing more materials, equipment, and supplies, you will need more room for storage and work space. Don't overlook the possibility of two separate work spaces, one such as a basement for pouring, molding, and messy procedures; the other, a finished room, for painting, decorating, packaging, etc., which are much cleaner jobs. You may have an extra room in the house that isn't being fully utilized, or you may pinch off a corner of a room used for some other purpose to finish candles. Your office space might be here, too.

You will need an office, of sorts. Your business is growing, and it's too large to get by with casual accounting, filing, and stocking procedures.

To stock your new office, I recommend the following things:

1. *Bulletin board or notebook* If you use a bulletin board, post each candle order in the order in which it will be completed. As you finish each item in the order, check it off and pack it for delivery. Or, if you are working on several orders at one time, make a list of the total number of each kind of candle you need, and as you make the candles, check them off on both the totaled sheet and the individual order sheet.

You will also want some record of how many candles and what styles and colors you have in stock. Keep this current to avoid confusion. You may also keep this type of information in a working notebook.

You'll need some other office supplies, such as a typewriter (handwritten letters don't make very good impressions or get very good results), invoices, packing slips, bills of lading, and price lists. Now might be a good time to have all of these items printed with the information on them that you desire, including your company name and address. But if you do not want to go to this expense, all the office supply stores carry these forms in stock, and for a dollar or two you can have rubber stamps made to put your name and address on them.

Some kind of filing system will have to be established. If you are fortunate enough to have a two or three-drawer filing cabinet, use that with a file folder for each company and sections for billing and correspondence.

If you don't have a filing cabinet, use shoe boxes or sweater boxes to keep your records sorted. Label each box, just as you would a file folder, and keep them all in one place so that things don't get lost.

Or you may want to buy a notebook with pockets in it for each classification in your file.

If you don't already have one, a telephone is almost a necessity in the Big Pot Stage. Besides the convenience of letting your fingers do the walking, you will also have a listing in the phone book, and this can mean money to you.

One day I received a call from a woman who had come to the Chicago Gift Show to buy for her shop. While she was there, she saw some of my candles in a store on Michigan Avenue. She tried to call me, but could find no listing for Deannie Candles. She finally persuaded the shop owner to tell her my name and phone number so that she could give me an order.

So a telephone can easily pay for itself, even if you don't advertise in the yellow pages. It's deductible on your income tax, too.

While you are getting the business procedures squared away, you may as well set up a company checking account. This will allow you to deposit checks made out to your company name, and it helps keep your records separate from household expenses. Shop around for a bank. They have widely different policies concerning business accounts. Choose the one that suits you best and costs you least.

Another business procedure to which you should direct your attention at this time is your company policy. You will need to establish definite policies under which you operate. For example: Do you offer discounts? What are your dealer terms? What is your minimum order? Do you require a certain number of each type and color of candle, or do you set a minimum dollar figure and sell any number of any color on or over that figure? I have always fixed a minimum dollar cost per order and allowed any number of any candle to come under that order.

If you sell any candles to out-of-town or out-of-state buyers, you will need definite freight policies. There are several possibilities here. Some companies make no freight allowances at all. Some companies allow a small percentage (2–5%) of the total amount of the order to apply to freight. Some companies pay all freight for any order over a certain figure such as $250 or $300. You may have some different ideas on this. Decide which one will work best for you, and then stay with it.

Another thing which merits some buying at this stage is packaging materials. You can only guess how many boxes of each size you will need, but there are some things you know you will always need, such as tissue paper, unprinted newspaper, tape, and tape dispenser, labels, brown wrapping paper, etc. I like to order reams and reams of tissue paper and cartons of tape, then that buying problem may not need attention for months.

A major item in the Big Pot Stage is transportation. It's nearly impossible to conduct a business of this size without your own transportation. If you have a family car, you certainly can utilize it for selling, small deliveries, and so forth. Then when you get really big orders, you may need to rent a truck to make the deliveries or to get the order to a commercial carrier.

It is also possible to lease a car or truck in the business' name, and write off the entire expense against the business. You should investigate this possibility to see if you qualify and if it's in your favor.

You will work out your own routine for this stage in your business, but I have found it very helpful to try to work a few hours every day, even if I don't have an order to fill. This gives me a head start on filling future orders, and it allows me some time to experiment in my candlecrafting.

Your buyers will always want new and different candles. If you can supply them, you will get orders to keep you just as busy as you wish to be.

Suppose that your business gets so big that you really can't handle the orders and fill them alone, but you need help. If you inquire about hiring people to work for you, you will probably discover that:

1. The person must be 16 years or older to work for you.

2. You must pay minimum hourly wages.

3. You must compute and deduct social security and withholding taxes from their wages and make periodic reports to the government and your employee.

4. You must increase your liability insurance to cover employees in your home.

5. You may be violating local ordinances and zoning restrictions.

Perhaps the solution to your problem lies in letting sub-contracts. There are any number of housewives who will gladly finish or package candles in their homes for an agreed-upon amount of money per candle, or do bookkeeping, etc. This way, they are self-employed, and you do not have to assume total responsibility for them as employees. You must make it worth their while, of course, and you should pay as much as you possibly can for their services. Also, you will have to get all the materials to them for assembling and packaging or whatever they are to do.

It is also possible to teach these "semi-employees" to completely make and package a candle for you. Sell them supplies at cost, and pay them all but 10 or 15¢ of what you will make on each candle.

There is another possibility for making money here, and that is to have other people participate in craft shows where they sell your candles. You might do it this way: Suppose that you find someone who will enter a craft show with your candles. They would have to pay the entry fees and attend the booth during the show, which means setting it up, selling, and returning unsold merchandise in new condition at the show's end.

You would provide them with a good assortment of candles. They would agree to pay you your wholesale cost per candle if the candles were sold, or to return any unsold candles to you in the same condition as when they left your shop. They may set their own prices at the shows (as this is hardly competition for any of your retailers) and they keep whatever profit they make over wholesale.

Another good possibility for making money in the Big Pot Stage is a mail-order candle. There are several steps involved in this process. As a matter of fact, I recommend that once you start the ball rolling on mail-order ads, you do nothing but that for several months.

First you must select a candle. It should meet most of the following qualifications:

1. It should be either exceptionally beautiful, very unusual, or both.
2. If possible, you should test-market it some to see how it sells.
3. It should be sturdy enough to withstand the professional manglers employed by the post office.
4. It should be small enough so that the cost of shipping it will not be exorbitant.
5. After you have chosen a suitable candle, you must decide where your best market will be.

Although this is pretty much a hunch, you might get some case histories of candles from the magazine or publications you are considering.

Our first mail order candle was Vladimir Voodoo, a do-it-yourself voodoo kit, complete with pins to stick into the candle. We felt that its appeal would be chiefly to the young people, and because the candle was to sell for $5, they would have to be affluent young people. Since fewer men buy candles than women, we decided that it should be a woman's magazine.

After some sleuthing and polling, we discovered that the female readers of *Cosmopolitan* magazine were chiefly young, well-educated, working girls in a high income bracket (over $10,000/year), who were big city dwellers, and that's where we decided to launch our mail order campaign.

Had we had a beautiful, decorative candle, or one which might appeal more to homemakers, we might have chosen a magazine such as *Better Homes and Gardens* or the like. Good common sense (and a bit of luck) is a good guide for selecting a mail-order marketplace.

Once the candle and the medium have been selected, you get down to the real nitty-gritty of the business. You must now price your candle fairly and reasonably.

Consider how much each candle costs in materials and supplies, packaging, labeling, etc. (don't forget you'll have to have mailing labels and keep VERY CAREFUL records on this candle, too). Then add your time (allow for some rejects) and postage costs.

By knowing the weight of each finished, packaged candle, you can find out from the post office department the minimum and the maximum postage to all zones. Add at least the average to your cost.

While you'll be making more profit per candle because you're selling at retail, you'll have some expenses that your retailer has always borne before such as bad debts, advertising, sales tax and keeping records on it, transportation, etc. With all these things in mind, decide on a price.

You will need a few other things in preparation for your venture. First of all, a post office box address is a sound idea. A box can be rented for just a few dollars a year, and then you have all of your mail orders separate from your other businesses.

If you don't already have one, a business checking account should be set up. It might even be worthwhile to have an account for ONLY this one candle. Some banks charge for every check which is deposited, and since you may be depositing thousands, you should make arrangements which exclude this charge. In our case, we keep a minimum balance of $100 and get no-charge checking.

Now you must place your ad. Write the magazine and tell them you want to place a mail-order ad. They'll send you all the necessary forms and information, plus some statistics on their circulation and case histories of other mail-order items—which may or may not have anything to do with candles. You'll have to supply them with a glossy photo (at least) and copy of your ad.

Suppose that you decide on a 70–71 line ad. This gives you a space about 5 inches x 2¼ inches. Besides the actual advertising space, you'll have to spend some money to have a picture of your candle made and to have copper engravings, etc., done. This can be handled by the magazine for an extra fee.

The copy for your ad can be a hand-done sketch like this:

DO IT YOURSELF VOODOO CANDLE

PICTURE

Is your boss a tryant? Did your steady put you down? Do you hate the government?

Witch doctors say that if you stick pins in or burn a wax image of your enemy, you will destroy him. So meet Vladimir Voodoo, complete with pins and ready to go up in smoke.

STICK A PIN! LIGHT A WICK! GET RID OF YOUR TROUBLES QUICK!

For your ppd. kit send $5 (check or m.o.) and your name and address to: Deannie Candles, P.O. Box 313, Arl. Hts., Ill. 60006

Make directions for ordering simple and concise. Read and reread your copy to be sure you haven't left out any vital information or given any ambiguous information. Ask for checks or money orders, and get any necessary papers to legalize checks made out to every conceivable variation of your company name.

The ad will have to be placed at *least* a couple of months before the time the magazine carrying it will come out, and because you're new and not yet established where credit is concerned, you'll be expected to accompany the order for the ad with a check to pay for it. They will probably give you a cash discount though, so maybe it won't smart too badly.

Now get ready and *go* on your candle.

Because you have no earthly idea how many you'll sell, you had better have at least 1,000 made up in advance and the capability for making thousands more quickly. Line up your "reserves" if you think it might be necessary to get help. If not, be double sure you can produce enough yourself to fill all orders promptly.

7
Manufacturer's Representatives

One day I got a telephone call from a gentleman who had seen my candles in one of the stores. He found them very different and to his liking, he said, and he would like to add our line of candles to his and sell them for us. He was, we discovered, a manufacturer's representative, or in other words, a salesman. We were intrigued by the idea, and business was a bit slow for us at the time, so we invited him over to discuss the matter. Some salesmen are hired by bigger companies to sell only that firm's products. A manufacturers rep, we learned, represents dozens, maybe even hundreds of small companies, and sells many different lines all rolled into one.

Our man, a very personable fellow, sells gifts, jewelry, and candles from numerous companies. He and two other salesmen sell the items over a four-state area. He calls on everything from tiny little boutiques to huge department store chains, keeps a showroom for all his wares, and exhibits in the big gift shows in four states.

He works on a commission basis, 20% of all he sells, and he does selling only. When he gets an order for us, he sends it to us. We fill it, ship it, and bill the store. His commission is paid on a given date, the month after the order is shipped, whether we are paid or not. Should an order be cancelled, it is called a charge-back, and he will pay his commission back to us for that order.

We showed him all the candles we can make and discussed prices, policies, packaging, freight allowances, billing, bookkeeping, and operating procedures. Then he asked us to get him three sets of samples, pictures of a standard size, and several hundred price lists for him to distribute as needed. Before we knew it, our first order had come in from him, and we were really in business.

At first we thought of having a sales rep as a luxury we couldn't really afford, but we think it's better to share some of your profits and sell more, than to try to do it all yourself and not sell as much.

We made two policy changes when we took on a rep. First we dropped our discounts to help pay for his commissions. The second change concerned freight. Rather than any of the previous ideas mentioned, we decided to pack all candles 13 to the dozen to defray freight expenses for the stores. In this way we did not pay our rep a commission on the freight allowance we were going to give back to the stores, our salesman could sell our candles easier by the dozen and not have to worry with figuring allowances, etc. The stores got the retail price of a candle back for every dozen they ordered (sometimes this amounts to more than what the freight cost them) and we're only out our cost on each extra candle. It has worked very well.

If you haven't already been approached by a rep, and would like to investigate the possibilities of having one, I suggest that you do one of two things. Either check the yellow pages of your local telephone directory and start calling likely companies, or ask some of your buyers if they know a local rep whom they like and trust.

I would think that the latter method would be more desirable, but I can see no reason why you could not select one on your own. I do suggest, however, that if you seek help without advice, that you ask for and check on references for whomever you ultimately choose.

Also, I strongly recommend that you have a firm written agreement between you concerning the responsibilities of each of you. There can be no room for disagreement if you both have a contract stating the terms and conditions under which you work.

8
How To Have Custom
Candle Molds

There are nearly an infinite number of possibilities for creating candles, and you can always buy molds and supplies from the professional designers and suppliers, but the day will undoubtedly come when you have an idea for a candle that is so outstanding and such a cinch to sell that you will want to make up your very own designs, molds, and candles.

Custom metal molds are the easiest, of course. You simply decide what size mold you want, etc., and then have a metalcraft company or one of the candle equipment manufacturing companies make the molds up to your specifications.

Plastic molds are something else again.

Let us suppose that you wish to make a Valentine candle. It is to be a representation of the earth, and it should look like a globe with all the continents in bas-relief. Around the center of this earth, you want the message "You mean the world to me."

First you must obtain a sculpture in either modeling clay, plaster, or wood that is an exact rendering of what your candle will look like. You may want to do this yourself or pay a sculptor or carver to do it for you. If you want a "pro" to do this for you, you'll have to find one. If there is a university or an art school near you, you may be able to get the names of teachers or students who would be willing to work with you. Or, if you have the time and the inclination, you can shop the galleries for an artist.

Another possibility is to go to some art and craft or sculpture shows and find an artist there. This is probably the best way, because you get to see their handiwork before you talk to them about your idea.

Whether you make the model yourself or have it made, always remember one thing. There must be no undercuts on the model, or your candle will not come out of the mold. Whatever is molded to the design, will have to be lifted straight up and off, and if there are little projections that will hold fast to the mold, your finished product will not release.

After you have your model for your candle, you will have to have a die made. Vacuum-formed plastic is simply a sheet of plastic material which is placed down over a die or design, and then heat and pressure are applied to shape the plastic into the form of the die. The die may be made of either epoxy or metal.

My suggestion is that you take your model to a vacuum-forming company and let them take it from here. They will have a die made and draw any specified number of molds in any kind of plastic, and they can give you an estimate of these costs before they proceed.

The estimates you get for this procedure may vary from $100 to $500 (for about 100 molds), and some companies need as much as six to eight months advance notice before they can deliver your finished candle molds to you. Shop around until you are satisfied that you have the best company for the best price.

After you have gone to this much trouble and expense, you will, of course, need to secure a copyright on the design. And you must make arrangements with the vacuum former to sell your molds to no one but you.

Do not show it to anyone or sell it until you have written to the Register of Copyrights, Library of Congress, Washington, D.C., for information on copyrights because if you "publish" it without the proper copyright notice, etc., the right to copyright is lost forever.

The copyright office will send you all the necessary forms and instructions for protecting your original candle from plagiarists. It will only cost you $6 and two copies of the work, and you may go ahead and sell while the copyright is being established just as long as you use the copyright notice as directed in their instructions.

Appendix

LIST OF SUPPLIERS

AMERICAN HANDICRAFTS
Contact General Offices 1011 Foch St., Ft. Worth, Texas 76107 for directory of stores and catalog.

BERSTED'S HOBBY CRAFT, INC.
521 West 10th Ave., Monmouth, Illinois

CALIFORNIA TITAN PRODUCTS, INC.
2501 S. Birch St., Santa Ana, California 92705

CUNNINGHAM ART PRODUCTS
1564 McCurdy Drive, Stone Mountain, Georgia 33083

DEEP FLEX PLASTIC MOLDS, INC.
A. 2740 Lipscomb St., P.O. Box 11471, Ft. Worth, Texas 76110
B. 803 Park Ave., P.O. Box 1257, Murfreesboro, Tennessee 37130

EMIX MANUFACTURING CO., INC.
Box 251, Parkersburg, West Virginia 26101

FITZGERALD ENTERPRISES, INC.
1610 E. 21st St., Oakland, California 94606

GLOW CANDLE CO.
P.O. Box 10102, Kansas City, Missouri 64111

HAZEL PEARSON HANDICRAFTS
P.O. Box 193, 4128 Temple City Blvd., Rosemead, California 91770

NATCOL CRAFTS
P.O. Box 299, Redlands, California

NOVELCRAFTS MANUFACTURING CO.
P.O. Box T, Rogue River, Oregon 97537

POURETTE MANUFACTURING CO.
6818 Roosevelt Way NE, Seattle, Washington 98115

PREMIER MFG. CO.
5862 Lamar, Arvada, Colorado 80002

W. T. ROGERS CO.
1309-11 W. Badger Rd., Madison, Wisconsin 53701

SUPPLEMENTARY READING MATERIAL ON CANDLECRAFTING

Berry, Conchita R. *Contemporary Candles.* Fort Worth: American Handicrafts, 1971.

Berry, Conchita R. *Romantic Candles.* Fort Worth: American Handicrafts, 1967.

Ferguson, Beverly. *Sculptured Wax.* Rosemead: Hazel Pearson Handicrafts, 1965 (Revised 1966).

Laklan, Carli. *The Candle Book.* New York: M. Burrows, 1956.

Monroe, Ruth. *Kitchen Candlecrafting.* South Brunswick and New York: A. S. Barnes and Company, 1970.

Newman, Thelma R. *Creative Candlemaking.* New York: Crown Publications, 1972.

Olsen, Don and Ray. *The Modern Art of Candle Creating.* South Brunswick and New York: A. S. Barnes and Company, 1963.

Schmidt, Clyde, Wynia and Russell. *Secrets of Candle Dipping.* Marshfield, Wisconsin: 1970.

Strose, Susanne. *Candlemaking.* New York: Sterling, 1968.

Index